Early Care & Education Practice

Level 5

Early Care & Education Practice

Level 5

Eilis Flood

and

Catriona Hardy

GILL EDUCATION

Gill Education
Hume Avenue
Park West
Dublin 12
www.gilleducation.ie

Gill Education is an imprint of M.H. Gill & Co.

© 2013 Eilis Flood and Catriona Hardy

978 07171 5844 7

Index compiled by Adam Pozner
Print origination by O'K Graphic Design, Dublin

The paper used in this book comes from the wood pulp of managed forests. For every tree felled, at least one tree is planted, thereby renewing natural resources.

For permission to reproduce photographs, the author and publisher gratefully acknowledge the following:

© Alamy: 70, 120; © Getty Images: 100, 126; Courtesy of Department of Children and Youth Affairs: 35; Courtesy of Department of Education and Skills: 76; Courtesy of Department of Health & Children: 49, 61.

The author and publisher have made every effort to trace all copyright holders, but if any has been inadvertently overlooked we would be pleased to make the necessary arrangement at the first opportunity.

Contents

Historical Development of the ECEC sector in Ireland

History of ECEC provision in Ireland

Pre-school education did not really exist in Ireland (apart from some exceptions) until the 1980s and 1990s. This was largely due to the fact that until quite recently the majority of Irish women did not work outside the home. Even if they did, childcare was usually provided by family members or childminders located in the community and known to the family. Irish policy discouraged women from working outside the home. The 'marriage bar' meant that women working in the public service had to leave their jobs as soon as they got married and become stay-at-home mothers and wives. This ban was lifted in 1957 for primary school teachers, but it was 1973 before the ban was lifted for other women in the public service.

Until recent years in Ireland, very few mothers worked outside the home. Therefore, there was little focus on pre-school education in Ireland until the late 1980s and 1990s. Most of the progress in the area of pre-school education in Ireland has come from the private rather than the public sector.

Outside the state-funded primary school system, investment in pre-school provision was traditionally targeted to support children in need of specific intervention, including educational disadvantage and children with special needs. The ECEC needs of babies, young children and their families were met instead by a broad range of community, voluntary and private enterprises. ECEC service provision was unregulated until 1997. When the Child Care (Pre-School) Regulations 2006 came into effect, no stipulation was made regarding the qualifications necessary to deliver such services beyond the person having their own children, a reference to show appropriate experience in caring for children and/or an appropriate qualification. Many services, especially those provided by the community and voluntary sector, relied heavily on volunteer staff. Even in the private sector, salaries were low and conditions of employment poor. Opportunities for employment in state-funded services were very limited (excluding primary teachers in infant classes) and similarly characterised by low status and low wages. Working in childcare was not generally viewed as a desirable career choice.

One important initiative came from the public sector in 1969, with the opening of a state-run pre-school in Rutland Street, Dublin. The Department of Education worked with the Van Leer Foundation – an organisation that promotes the early education of children living in economically disadvantaged areas. Together, they set up the pre-school in Rutland Street as a template for other such pre-schools around the country. These pre-schools were known as Early Start pre-schools. A total of 40 pre-schools opened nationally – all of which are still open today. The aim of these pre-schools is to combat the effects of economic and social disadvantage on educational achievement. This is achieved by giving children a good start to their education.

In 1992, Ireland ratified the United Nations Convention on the Rights of the Child. This helped to bring to public consciousness the rights of children. And in 2000, the Department of Health and Children published the National Children's Strategy. This strategy set out a ten-year plan for the improvement of children's lives in Ireland. The strategy document stated that its vision was for:

> An Ireland where children are respected as young citizens with a valued contribution to make and a voice of their own; where all children are cherished and supported by family and the wider society; where they enjoy a fulfilling childhood and realise their potential... (DoHC 2000: 10)

One of the goals of the National Children's Strategy is that 'children will receive quality supports and services to promote all aspects of their development' (DoHC 2000: 30). The strategy aims to fulfil this by providing quality childcare services and family-friendly employment measures.

There have been many other significant initiatives and decisions in Ireland in recent years in an attempt to respond to the demand for quality in ECEC.

National Forum on Early Childhood Education (1998)

The National Forum on Early Childhood Education was established in 1998 by the then Minister for Education and Science, Micheál Martin. The forum brought together organisations and individuals with an interest in early childhood education, and in this way it created a 'think tank' from which a number of very worthwhile initiatives came, e.g. the White Paper on Early Childhood Education, *Ready to Learn* (DES 1999).

National Voluntary Childcare Collaborative (1999)

The National Voluntary Childcare Collaborative (NVCC) was first established in 1999. Today, the organisation comprises seven national non-governmental agencies dedicated to the promotion of ECEC in Ireland. While the organisations involved are non-governmental, the NVCC can receive government funding. The seven organisations involved in the NVCC are:

- Barnardos
- Childminding Ireland
- Children in Hospital Ireland
- Forbairt Naíonraí Teo
- Early Childhood Ireland
- Irish Steiner Kindergarten Association
- St Nicholas Montessori Society of Ireland.

These organisations aim to continue the work of the past number of decades by promoting ECEC in Ireland.

White Paper on Early Childhood Education, Ready to Learn (1999)

The purpose of this White Paper was to set out government policy on all issues relating to early childhood education. Quality of provision was the key theme of the White Paper. It recognised that while there was much quality provision in the ECEC sector, there was also a need to standardise provision. These findings led directly to the Child Care Pre-School Regulations (DoHC 2006), Síolta (CECDE 2006) and Aistear (NCCA 2009). All three of these initiatives are concerned with standardisation and quality of provision.

Centre for Early Childhood Development and Education (2002)

The Centre for Early Childhood Development and Education (CECDE) was established by Dublin Institute of Technology and St Patrick's College, Drumcondra. It was launched by the Minister for Education and Science in 2002. CECDE aimed to achieve the goals set out in *Ready to Learn* (1999). The organisation was disbanded in 2008, when it was seen by government to have achieved everything it was set up to do. Among other things, CECDE produced Ireland's first quality framework, entitled *Síolta: The National Quality Framework for Early Childhood Education* (2006).

Child Care (Pre-School) Regulations 2006

Child Care (Pre-School Services) (No 2) Regulations 2006 was produced by the Department of Health and Children. This document set out pre-school regulations and put on a statutory basis ECEC service provision in Ireland. The regulations clearly list all the requirements that must be met by organisations or individuals providing ECEC services to children aged 0–6. The regulations cover such issues as first aid, management, staff–child ratios, behaviour management, fire safety measures, premises and facilities, heating, ventilation, lighting, facilities for rest and play, etc.

Fulfilment of the requirements of these regulations undoubtedly put much work and expense on ECEC providers, particularly those providing services from premises that were not purpose built. Having said this, many people believe that these regulations have done more than any other initiative for the improvement of ECEC services for children. This is because they are on a statutory footing and they are enforced by HSE inspectors.

Síolta (2006)

The Department of Education and Skills published *Síolta: The National Quality Framework for Early Childhood Education* in 2006. The Síolta framework was developed by CECDE in a process that took over three years and involved more than 50 different organisations representing childcare workers, teachers, parents, policymakers and researchers. Síolta aims to define, assess and support the improvement of quality across all aspects of practice in ECEC settings that cater for children aged 0–6. Settings covered by Síolta include full- and part-time day care, childminding services and sessional services, e.g. Montessori classrooms and infant classes in primary schools.

The inclusion of infant classes in primary schools represents a new departure for ECEC in Ireland. Up until the publication of Síolta (and Aistear in 2009), pre-school and primary school children were treated very differently. It is now understood that children aged 0–6 require a developmental-based (as opposed to subject-based) curriculum regardless of whether the child is in pre-school or primary school. Since December 2008 (after CECDE was disbanded), the Early Years Education Policy Unit in the Department of Education and Skills has been responsible for the implementation of Síolta.

Aistear (2009)

Up until recent years, the curriculum followed by pre-school settings was largely undirected and unregulated. This has inevitably resulted in variation in the quality of the curriculum provided by settings. In 1999, the NCCA published the *Primary School Curriculum*, which did direct and regulate the curriculum followed in infant classes. However, in 2004 the OECD conducted its *Thematic Review of Early Childhood Education and Care Policy in Ireland*. This review found that education provided in infant classes in primary schools in Ireland was too directive and formal (OECD 2004: 58).

In 2009, the NCCA published *Aistear: The Early Childhood Curriculum Framework*. The ultimate aim of Aistear is the development of the whole child. This is in contrast with the previous Primary School Curriculum, which was more subject based. Infant classes in primary schools must now follow the Aistear curriculum. This is a huge departure for ECEC in Ireland. For years, Scandinavian countries have been using curricula similar to Aistear and it is now understood that introducing children to formal, direct education at too young an age is counterproductive and can suppress children's natural enthusiasm and curiosity for learning. American educator John Holt (1923–85) devoted much of his time to researching this topic.

It is important to note that (at the time of writing) Aistear is inspected in primary school settings only. It is not inspected in pre-school settings, which may have reduced its impact.

Free Pre-School Year Programme

In 2010, the Department of Children and Youth Affairs introduced the Free Pre-School Year in Early Childhood Care and Education Programme. Before this, it was only children in disadvantaged areas who could avail of free or subsidised pre-school education. The Free Pre-School Year Programme recognises that *all* children benefit from quality pre-school education. The programme recognises that because pre-school education in Ireland usually comes from private providers, it is expensive and therefore not available to all children, e.g. children of parents not working outside the home. Under the programme, pre-school providers are paid per child enrolled. The providers must meet certain criteria before entering the scheme, e.g. staff qualifications. This has had the effect of incentivising providers to meet criteria, which in turn has increased the quality of provision.

ECEC Services Currently Available in Ireland

The types of ECEC services currently available in Ireland can be organised under these headings:
- Sessional services, which provide ECEC services for a set period of time during the day (e.g. 9am–1pm)
- Full-time services, which provide ECEC services throughout the day.
- Part-time services, which provide ECEC services for a total of more than 3.5 hours and less than 5 hours a day. It may include a sessional pre-school service for pre-school children not attending the part-time day care service.

Up to 80 per cent of services in Ireland, whether sessional or full time, are owned and operated by the private sector. All registered services (regardless of who operates or funds them) must comply with the Child Care (Pre-School) Regulations 2006 and they must also follow the Síolta and Aistear frameworks.

Sessional Services

Playgroups

Playgroups operate in a range of settings and are usually open for approximately three hours per day. Children usually attend playgroups from the age of two-and-a-half until they go to primary school. Some playgroups are privately owned. *Community playgroups* are primarily funded by government and are run by community members. Many community playgroups are staffed by individuals on government employment schemes, e.g. Community Employment Scheme (CE). These staff members are encouraged to undertake further education and training.

Montessori Schools

Usually, Montessori pre-schools are privately owned and they operate for approximately three hours per day. Some Montessori schools run two sessions (morning and afternoon), with children attending one session per day. Montessori pre-schools are run according to the principles and educational methods of Maria Montessori. While Montessori pre-schools in Ireland do follow the Aistear framework, they also learn via the Montessori curriculum and practical materials.

Naíonraí

Naíonraí are pre-schools run through the medium of the Irish language. They are supported by an organisation called Forbairt Naíonraí Teoranta and there are almost 200 of them nationwide. Naíonraí also follow the Aistear framework, of which there is an Irish-language version. Children between the ages three and five attend for approximately three hours.

Early Start

The Early Start Programme is a one-year preventative intervention scheme offered in selected pre-schools in designated disadvantaged areas. The objective of the pre-school programme, which is managed and funded by the Department of Education and Skills, is to tackle educational disadvantage by targeting children who are at risk of not reaching their potential within the school system. The Early Start Pre-School Programme was introduced in 1994 in eight pilot schools in disadvantaged areas. It expanded the following year to 40 schools and now caters for over 1,650 children in Ireland. Most schools are located in the Dublin area, with 26 schools there. There are six schools in Cork and three in Limerick. There is one each in Galway, Waterford, Bray (Co. Wicklow), Dundalk (Co. Louth) and Drogheda (Co. Louth). Early Start implements the Aistear framework in an effort to enhance the overall development of young children and to prevent school failure by trying to counteract the effects of social disadvantage.

Pre-schools for Traveller Children

Up to recently, funding was provided for a number of pre-schools that catered specifically for Traveller children who might not otherwise have been able to avail of a pre-school year. However, since the introduction of the Free Pre-School Year Programme in 2010, all children can avail of one year's free pre-school, so there is no longer separate provision for Traveller children.

Pre-schools for Children with Special Needs

Local Health Offices and/or voluntary bodies provide services for young children with severe or profound disabilities. Services are provided in specialised centres around the country and are generally run by a clinical director and staffed by nurses with an intellectual disability qualification, ECEC trained teachers and often play therapists. While pre-school children in Ireland do not have a specific right to education, they are entitled to certain health services that are related to education.

The Health Service Executive (HSE) is responsible for providing psychological services and speech and language therapy services for pre-school children with disabilities who are assessed as needing these services. Assessments of children under 5 are carried out under the 'assessment of need' provisions of the Disability Act 2005. The Visiting Teacher Service of the Department of Education and Skills (DES) provides a service to young children with visual and/or hearing impairment, from the age of 2.

There are a small number of special pre-school class units for children with autistic spectrum disorders. These units are sometimes attached to primary schools. There are also a number of ABA schools in Ireland. These schools cater for children with autism by using a specific method of teaching called **A**pplied **B**ehavioural **A**nalysis.

Parent and Toddler Groups

These are informal groups where babies and toddlers go with their parents to meet other babies, toddlers and parents. They are aimed at providing play and socialisation opportunities for children and they normally take place in settings such as community centres or parents' homes. Parent and toddler groups are supported by Early Childhood Ireland.

Full-time Services

Crèches, Day Care Centres and Nurseries

These terms are used to describe services offering full-time care and education for babies and children. Services are usually provided for children aged 6 months to school-going age. Childcare regulations state that the adult–baby ratio must not exceed 1:3; this ratio increases to 1:5 for babies aged over 12 months. Because of this, many settings will not accept children under the age of 12 months.

Many facilities also offer afterschool care and/or homework clubs for primary school children. This means that crèches, day care centres and nurseries now cater for children aged 6 months to 12 years. While most full-time services are privately owned and funded by parental fees, a small number are government funded, i.e. community crèches. Some large employers and also many of the larger colleges and universities provide crèche facilities at subsidised rates for their staff and students. These services usually operate a long day (8am–6pm) to facilitate working parents. Some city crèches open as early as 6am.

Family Day Care/Childminders

This is the most common form of ECEC service in Ireland. According to Childminding Ireland (2012), approximately 70 per cent of children in out-of-home settings are cared for in this way. It is estimated that there are approximately 37,900 childminders working in Ireland today (National Childcare Strategy 2006). Childminders who care for three or fewer children are exempt from the Child Care (Pre-School) Regulations 2006. However, they are encouraged to register voluntarily with their local Childminder Advisory Officer (CMO), whose name and contact details are available through the local City/County Childcare Committee (CCC). Under the Childcare Act 1991, childminders caring for more than three pre-school children are required to register with the HSE. However, many do not do this.

All childminders (whether registered or not) are encouraged to follow the National Guidelines for Childminders, which were published by the Office of the Minister for Children in 2006 and updated in 2008. Recent government initiatives have tried to regulate this area by offering a number of different incentives to childminders who register their service. These incentives include training by CCCs; financial supports, e.g. childminding development grant (€1000) and capital grants (up to €75,000); and tax exemptions, i.e. childminders can earn up to €15,000 per year tax free. If childminders register, they are included on the CCC list of registered providers. This can be a useful way of advertising childminding services, since many new parents look to the list of registered providers when investigating childcare options.

Occupations within the Childcare Sector

- **Nursery nurses**

  These practitioners provide care for children in day or residential nurseries, children's homes, maternity units and similar establishments. Related job titles include crèche assistant, nursery assistant and nursery nurse.

- **Playgroup leaders**

  These practitioners deliver and facilitate play opportunities for children in a range of formal and informal settings, including play groups, play schemes, free play locations and after-school activities. Related job titles include play leader and playgroup assistant.

- **Educational/Special Needs assistants**
  These practitioners assist teachers with (or relieve them of) a variety of non-teaching duties. Related job titles include classroom helper, education care officer, non-teaching assistant, school helper and special needs assistant.
- **Childcare manager/supervisor**
  These practitioners ensure that the care and education of the children is being maintained at all times. They take care of any issues that arise and they are in direct contact with parents. They are responsible for the day-to-day running of the childcare facility. This role requires childcare qualifications as well as experience in the area. The role also requires excellent interpersonal and organisation skills and the ability to manage a team of employees.
- **Montessori teacher**
  These practitioners ensure efficient day-to-day running of a Montessori education setting. They follow Montessori guidelines regarding the education of young children. They present different exercises to children using the Montessori materials and they practise observation on a regular basis.
- **Other childcare and related occupations**
  There are many other childcare practitioners who perform a variety of domestic activities in the day-to-day care of children. They supervise and participate in children's play, education and other activities. Related job titles include childminder, nanny and au pair.

City/County Childcare Committees (CCCs)

There are 33 City/County Childcare Committees (CCCs) that were established in 2001 to encourage and facilitate the development of childcare locally. They provide information and advice on setting up your own business in the childcare sector, training courses for people interested in working in the childcare sector and useful information for parents about local childcare facilities.

In Budget 2006, the Irish government announced the establishment of the National Childcare Investment Programme 2006–2010 (NCIP), which succeeded the previous earlier Equal Opportunities Childcare Programme. City/County Childcare Committees are open to members of the public who wish to apply for grant assistance and support information under the National Childcare Investment Programme.

List of City/County Childcare Committees	
Carlow	Limerick County
Cavan	Longford
Clare	Louth
Cork City	Mayo
Cork County	Meath
Donegal	Monaghan
Dublin City	Offaly
Dublin South	Roscommon
Dun Laoghaire	Sligo
Fingal	Tipperary North
Galway	Tipperary South
Kerry	Waterford City
Kildare	Waterford County
Kilkenny	Westmeath
Laois	Wexford
Leitrim	Wicklow
Limerick City	

Public Health Nurses

The Public Health Nurse is employed by the HSE. Their role is to serve the community with a range of healthcare services; they are also registered general nurses. They are usually based within the community and will cover certain local areas. They may visit schools. They may visit elderly people who require help to dress a wound. They also visit newborn babies and their mothers within a six-week period of them being discharged from hospital. Public Health Nurses engage in regular contact with GPs, hospitals and other healthcare providers about a patient in their care. This will ensure that the other healthcare providers have up-to-date knowledge so that they can ensure best practice.

Special Needs Assistants

Special Needs Assistants (SNAs) are employed to facilitate learners with a disability related to education. SNAs may work in a special school or in mainstream schools either on a part-time or full-time basis, as mentioned earlier. They take on a non-teaching role and are always under the supervision of the class teacher. An SNA may help a child to get on and off buses. They may help the child with reading and writing exercises. They may also help with feeding and toileting. SNAs are required to have an appropriate qualification to work as a special needs assistant, e.g. level 5 course in Special Needs Assisting.

Primary Teachers

Primary school teachers are qualified to teach the primary school curriculum to children aged 4–12. Primary school teachers have a number of important roles. They ensure the social and academic development of the children in their care. They plan and deliver lessons within the primary school curriculum and they have regular interaction with parents and guardians.

Educational Psychologists

The role of the educational psychologist is to assess the needs of children and young people who have problems relating to behaviour, learning and/or social/emotional development. This may be done by observing and/or interviewing the child. The appropriate methods of helping the child will then be established, e.g. different therapies, counselling or learning support programmes. Educational psychologists work in many different settings, within schools, the HSE, private practices and third-level institutions.

Family Support Workers

The Family Support Worker Service offers practical and emotional support to families if it is required. The aim of this service is to ensure where possible that children remain with their families. This service also offers home-based support to families for a certain number of hours per week. The support services include parenting skills, information on diet, nutrition and healthcare, budgeting and family finance, and confidence and personal development. If the family support worker has concerns regarding the family, they will report this information to a social worker.

Social Workers

The social worker in childcare services can work in four main areas: child protection, child placement, child and adolescent psychiatry, and family support. Social workers often work with families and individuals that require support with a number of problems, e.g. emotional, social, psychiatric and behavioural. They may also work with individuals and their families on a regular basis regarding issues such as child abuse and domestic violence.

Childcare Organisations and Non-governmental Agencies

Barnardos

Barnardos children's charity delivers a variety of services and works in close proximity with children and their families depending on their specific needs. The aim of this is to promote family learning and development and, therefore, to enhance the family's overall wellbeing.

Barnardos strives to give children positive childhood experiences:

> If a child's learning and development, and his or her emotional wellbeing, is successfully and measurably improved through our work, then the child's ability to benefit from life opportunities and manage life challenges will be improved, and therefore the path of his or her life will be changed for the better. (www.barnardos.ie)

Barnardos aims to improve government laws, policies and procedures across all areas that affect children's lives. They do this by ensuring that the knowledge and experience they gain through working with children and their families in areas such as education and health is heard at government level. They also engage in regular political meetings with government and opposition parties and relevant policy makers.

There are a number of ways in which people can learn about the work of Barnardos: internet, posters, billboards, media interviews and articles.

Barnardos offers services across three stages of child development:

- Children aged 0–5 ('best start')
- Children aged 6–12 ('best chance')
- Children and young people aged 13–18 ('best choice').

Barnardos may work with a child's family in order for the child to experience a happy family life with good relationships with parents and siblings. This work may include:

- Providing group sessions with parents and children to practise skills such as listening and problem-solving skills
- Providing help and advice to parents in different areas, e.g. managing challenging behaviour
- Engaging with children of different ages on relevant and often sensitive issues, e.g. a family that has been affected by alcohol misuse
- Providing a *guardian ad litem*: a person who is qualified and experienced in working with children that are involved in family law proceedings. This service gives the child involved an independent voice in court. This person can speak on the child's behalf and explain what the child's particular wishes are. The *guardian ad litem* works in conjunction with the child's family at all times.
- Providing an *origin tracing service*, which is especially for people who spent some or all of their childhood growing up in an Irish industrial school. This confidential service provides them with the necessary assistance in finding information relating to any of their relatives. Staff who deliver this service are highly trained.

- Providing a confidential *post adoption service* for adults, e.g. a helpline number or e-mail service for birth family and adoptive family members. A mediation service is available for people who were adopted and have come in contact with birth relatives and want to begin correspondence. There are training and support meetings for parents who have adopted children from various countries outside of Ireland. The service may also be useful for adoptive parents to discuss any questions they may have about their adult adoptive child seeking birth relatives. Adoptive parents are also welcome to contact the service to discuss any questions or anxieties they might have about their adult son or daughter making contact with birth relatives.

Barnardos provides a range of *parenting programmes and talks*. These are designed for parents of children of every age (0–18). These programmes can offer support to parents in managing their child's needs and in understanding their child. Topics will be selected to address the needs of the parents and their child's stage of development.

    Teen parent programmes are another important part of the work of Barnardos. In these programmes, Barnardos works in careful collaboration with teenage parents, both male and female, together with their children to assist them with advice on financial/educational support.

Services Provided to the Community

Barnardos works with children in disadvantaged areas. They provide many services, including the following.

- **Early Years/Tús Maith services**

These are programmes suitable for children aged 0–5. The main principle is to support children and to manage their transition into primary school. This programme works using the HighScope approach, where children have direct experiences based on their own interests and ideas, along with a programme called the REDI programme (**re**search-based, **d**evelopmentally **i**nformed).

- **Friendship group**

Barnardos realises the importance of children having friends (particularly friends of the same age). Therefore, they offer a friendship group which facilitates children in learning the necessary skills to establish genuine and meaningful relationships. These friendship groups are typically suited for children aged 6–9. Each group is made up of six children and two staff who meet every week for two hours over a period of weeks.

- **Vetting service**

Barnardos provides a vetting service that assists in the processing of Garda vetting applications for a number of groups/organisations that are not directly registered with the Garda Central Vetting Unit. This is at the request of (and in collaboration with) the Department of Children and Youth Affairs (DCYA).

■ **Wizards of Words**

Barnardos provides a service known as Wizards of Words (WoW). The programme is a paired literacy improvement programme. It is suitable for children in first and second class in primary school. The programme delivers one-to-one tuition with older volunteers during school time and on the school premises. The trained volunteers (who are typically aged 55 and over) meet with children who have been nominated by the teacher, three times a week during school hours. The volunteers provide reading support to the children. Barnardos appoints a project leader who trains and supports the volunteers in the implementation of the programme, monitors progress and ensures that the programme is run effectively. WoW is currently hosted in eight schools in Dublin and Limerick.

■ **Training and consultancy**

Barnardos offers training to childcare professionals, parents and all people that work in the childcare area. The training given is within the important context of Síolta, the National Quality Framework.

■ **Bereavement counselling**

Barnardos has a bereavement counselling service for children and young people who have lost someone close to them. They try to help them through the grieving process and give them the opportunity to talk. Counsellors are based in Cork and Dublin, but work with children from across the country.

Childminding Ireland

Childminding Ireland aims to promote quality childminding as a beneficial form of non-parental care for children of all ages, from infancy to school-age. Childminding Ireland explains that childminders are dedicated to offering constant care in small, home-like settings in which children are most comfortable.

> Childminding Ireland, as the National Association, is committed to promoting the development of quality in family-based care for children by providing a range of services for childminders, promoting Síolta quality standards, developing training for the childminding sector and promoting the development of local childminding networks. (www.childmindingireland.ie)

Childminding Ireland has a number of objectives in relation to childcare. They aim to:

■ Promote high-quality ECEC standards for children and ensure that all their developmental needs are met
■ Support and advise childminders and parents in the area of ECEC
■ Maintain a code of standards for family-based care for children
■ Encourage the recognition of childminding as a positive care facility for young children.

Childminding Ireland strives to ensure that that their knowledge is heard at government level; they have direct contact with the Minister for Children and the officials who design policies that are directly linked to childminding. Childminding Ireland is constantly lobbying to change and improve laws, policies and procedures in the relevant areas. They often attend meetings with both government and opposition public representatives. They promote public awareness for childminders in many ways, e.g. providing an up-to-date and easily accessible website, along with print articles.

Childminders are always welcome to register with Childminding Ireland. In doing so, they can enjoy many benefits. There is free advertising on the Childminding Ireland website (www.childminding.ie). The website also offers other useful resources, including sample policies and procedures, and information on upcoming training courses and local events. Childminding Ireland also operates a telephone helpline, which is open five days a week.

Forbairt Naíonraí Teoranta

Forbairt Naíonraí Teoranta (www.naíonraí.ie) is an all-Ireland voluntary organisation that supports the promotion of education and care services in Irish for children from birth onwards. Children learning through Irish attend a Naíonra and are taught solely through Irish.

- Forbairt Naíonraí Teoranta provides a number of services through Irish: afterschool care, summer camps, and parent/guardian and toddler groups.
- Forbairt Naíonraí Teoranta offers advice and assistance to parents who wish to send their children to a Naíonra. They also offer support for new and existing Naíonraí. There is a grant scheme open to all Naíonraí outside the Gaeltacht regions.
- Forbairt Naíonraí Teoranta is a QQI-recognised training centre and it provides intensive training courses in Childcare Levels 5 and 6.

    There is a wide range of material and books available from Forbairt Naíonraí Teoranta and they also provide some basic equipment suitable for a Naíonra. Forbairt Naíonraí Teoranta publishes a monthly newsletter containing information and articles of interest to all involved in childcare.

Irish Steiner Kindergarten Association

The Irish Steiner Kindergarten Association (www.steinerireland.org) is Ireland's main source of information on Steiner Waldorf education. The organisation provides support for members who are based all around Ireland.

The organisation was formed in 1992. Initially, membership was restricted to those who were working in a Steiner kindergarten and, since Steiner education was unfamiliar at the time in Ireland, there was little interest from those outside the area. However, in recent years there has been an increasing recognition of many different pre-school methodologies. Steiner

Waldorf education has become more popular in Ireland and there is greater recognition of its importance in children's development.

The Irish Steiner Kindergarten Association has a number of objectives in relation to childcare. They aim to:

- Promote and support the development of Steiner Waldorf ECEC in Ireland
- Represent professionals working in Steiner Waldorf schools in Ireland
- Establish and develop a range of training programmes for childcare practitioners
- Provide professional in-service training programmes for members. The association has established a programme of training workshops on aspects of Steiner Waldorf education for childcare professionals.
- Collaborate with other organisations and agencies to promote high-quality, affordable childcare services in the community.

St Nicholas Montessori Society of Ireland

St Nicholas Montessori Society of Ireland (www.montessoriireland.ie) provides certification of Montessori pre-school programmes which ensure that Montessori pre-schools are of the highest possible standard. As there are no set standards which Montessori schools must adhere to, St Nicholas Montessori Society of Ireland have set out their own standards. Montessori schools that wish to register with the organisation must satisfy these standards. These standards require, for example, that Montessori teachers have the appropriate Montessori qualifications and that they attend St Nicholas Montessori Society of Ireland's workshop/refresher course during the year. The Montessori pre-school must adhere to the Child Care (Pre-School) Regulations 2006. The Montessori classroom must be purpose built and must be complete with a wide range of Montessori materials.

There are many benefits for Montessori pre-schools that register with the society.

- Since registered schools must follow the principles of Maria Montessori, this helps to set and raise standards of Montessori education in Ireland.
- Montessori Education Mentors help Montessori teachers in all areas of the Montessori approach to education.
- The society provides information on training, refresher courses and workshops.
- Registered pre-schools are given unlimited access to the society's website, which is regularly updated with useful information.

Early Childhood Ireland

Early Childhood Ireland (www.earlychildhoodireland.ie) represents and supports individuals who are in any way involved in the development, delivery and oversight of ECEC in Ireland. Early Childhood Ireland is a member organisation. It has more than 3,200 members and is open to people in the childcare area, including managers and staff of ECEC settings, employees in the childcare sector, students of childcare, parents and relatives of children, and researchers and policy makers who influence the quality, availability and range of ECEC services.

Early Childhood Ireland has a number of objectives in relation to childcare. They aim to:

- Provide professional support and training for ECEC practitioners
- Contribute to research and public policy development
- Promote best-quality ECEC that is accessible to all children
- Explore and evaluate different child-centered approaches to ECEC.

Children in Hospital Ireland

Children in Hospital Ireland is a voluntary organisation that ensures children in hospital receive the best possible care. They also promote the care of children's families.

2

Legislation, Policies, Practices and Procedures

UN Convention on the Rights of the Child (1989)

The United Nations Convention on the Rights of the Child (UNCRC) is an internationally binding agreement on the rights of children, adopted by the UN General Assembly in 1989. A child is defined in the UNCRC as a person under the age of 18. Ireland signed the convention on 30 September 1990 and ratified it on 28 September 1992. By ratifying the convention, the Irish state committed itself to the promotion, protection and fulfilment of children's rights as outlined by the convention. The convention incorporates children's rights under three categories:

- Civil and political (e.g. their treatment under the law)
- Social, economic and cultural (e.g. an adequate standard of living)
- Protection (e.g. protection from abuse and exploitation).

Children's Referendum 2012

Every five years the progress of countries that have ratified the UNCRC is monitored and reviewed. A plan is then put in place to assist any countries that need to improve their provision. While Ireland did make progress after ratifying the UNCRC in 1992 (e.g. establishing a new government department for Children and Youth Affairs), a significant problem existed. Under Irish domestic law, children were almost 'invisible', having no specific rights as children in our constitution. In this way the Irish constitution has not been compatible with the principles and provisions of the UNCRC. The Children's Referendum, passed on 10 November 2012, sought to improve aspects of Ireland's constitution by inserting a new article. The new article is 42A. It is to be inserted between articles 42 and 43 and it will remove the old article 42.5.

Article 42A consists of four sections.

- **Section 1**

  'The state recognises and affirms the natural and imprescriptible rights of all children and shall, as far as practicable, by its laws protect and vindicate those rights.'

- **Section 2**

  'In exceptional cases, where the parents, regardless of their marital status, fail in their duty towards their children to such extent that the safety or welfare of any of their children is likely to be prejudicially affected, the state as guardian of the common good shall, by proportionate means as provided by law, endeavour to supply the place of the parents, but always with due regard for the natural and imprescriptible rights of the child.

  'Provision shall be made by law for the adoption of any child where the parents have failed for such a period of time as may be prescribed by law in their duty towards the child and where the best interests of the child so require.'

Section 3

'Provision shall be made by law for the voluntary placement for adoption and the adoption of any child.'

Section 4

- 'Provision shall be made by law that in the resolution of all proceedings:
  1 brought by the state, as guardian of the common good, for the purpose of preventing the safety and welfare of any child from being prejudicially affected, or
  2 concerning the adoption, guardianship or custody of, or access to, any child, the best interests of the child shall be the paramount consideration.
- 'Provision shall be made by law for securing, as far as practicable, that in all proceedings referred to in subsection 1° of this section in respect of any child who is capable of forming his or her own views, the views of the child shall be ascertained and given due weight having regard to the age and maturity of the child.'

This change to the Irish constitution has considerable implications for children in care and children who are currently living within their family unit but are at risk of abuse and neglect (or are already experiencing abuse or neglect). The state has a duty to intervene in such cases, removing such children from their families if this is considered to be in their best interests. If the parents of such children do not 'clean up their act', so to speak, within a period stipulated by the law, it is within the rights of the state to allow such children to be adopted if this is considered to be in the children's best interests. In the past, consent had to be given by biological parents for a child to be adopted in this country. This has meant that many children living in loving foster homes have been not been adopted by their foster parents because their biological parents have not consented. Children in foster care must now be listened to and their wishes taken into account with regard to decisions made about them. The wishes of children who are the subject of guardianship or custody battles must now also be considered before decisions are taken.

Structure of the UNCRC

The UNCRC sets out children's rights in 54 *articles* (articles 43–54 explain how the government ensures articles relate to all children). The convention sets out a number of *guiding principles*, which are divided into four *core principles*.

Guiding principles

The guiding principles are general requirements for all rights.

■   **Definition of the child (Article 1)**

The convention defines a 'child' as a person younger than 18 years of age, unless the laws of a particular country lower the legal age for adulthood. The Committee on the Rights of the Child is the monitoring body for the convention. It has encouraged states to review the age of majority if it is set below 18 and to increase the level of protection for all children under 18.

■   **Non-discrimination (Article 2)**

The convention applies to all children, regardless of race, religion, abilities, beliefs or family background. It doesn't matter where children live, what language they speak, whether they are male or female, what their culture is, whether they have a disability or whether they are rich or poor. No child should be treated unfairly on any grounds.

■   **Best interests of the child (Article 3)**

The best interests of children must be the primary concern when making a decision that may affect them, whether it seems big or small. All adults should do what is best for children. When adults make decisions, they should think about how their decisions will affect the children in their care.

■   **Right to life, survival and development (Article 6)**

Children have the right to live. States should ensure that children survive and develop healthily.

■   **Respect for the views of the child (Article 12)**

When adults are making decisions that affect children, children have the right to say what they think should happen and to have their opinions taken into account. The convention is aware that a child's participation in decision-making is in accordance with their level of maturity.

Core Principles

Within the UNCRC, the rights of the child can be classified under the following four headings:
■   Survival
■   Development
■   Protection
■   Participation.

Survival and Development

The rights of the child in relation to survival and development are those things that are deemed necessary for a healthy life. They include rights to food, shelter, water, education, primary healthcare, leisure and recreation, cultural activities and information about rights.

■ **Article 4: Protection of rights**

Governments have a responsibility to take the necessary measures to ensure that children's rights are respected and fulfilled. This involves assessing their social services, legal, health and educational systems, as well as levels of funding for these services. They must help families protect children's rights and create an environment where children can grow and reach their potential. In some instances, this may involve changing existing laws or creating new ones.

■ **Article 5: Parental guidance**

The state should respect the rights and responsibilities of families to direct and guide their children. The state does not take rights and responsibilities away from parents; it assists them in fulfilling such important roles.

■ **Article 6: Survival and development**

Children have the right to live. The state should ensure that children survive and develop healthily.

■ **Article 7: Registration, name, nationality and care**

All children have the right to a legally registered name, which is recognised by the state. Children have the right to a nationality and ideally they should be cared for by their parents.

■ **Article 8: Preservation of identity**

Children have the right to an identity. The state should respect children's right to a name.

■ **Article 9: Separation from parents**

The state should recognise that children have the right to live with their parents and should not be separated from them against their will, except when it is subject to a judicial review and separation is in the best interests of the child (e.g. in a case of abuse or neglect). Children whose parents do not live together have the right to stay in contact with both parents, unless this might hurt the child.

■ **Article 10: Family reunification**

Families whose members live in another country should be allowed to move between those countries so that parents and children can stay in contact or get back together as a family.

■ Article 14: Freedom of thought, conscience and religion

The state must respect the right of the child to freedom of thought, conscience and religion. The convention respects the rights and duties of parents in providing religious and moral guidance to their children. Children have the right to examine and practise their religion, as long as they respect other people while doing so. The convention recognises that when children mature they will form their own views; some may question certain religious practices or cultural traditions.

■ Article 18: Parental responsibilities and state assistance

Both parents (or legal guardians, as the case may be) have equal responsibility for the upbringing of their children. Governments respect this responsibility and therefore provide the necessary assistance to parents. The state shall ensure the development of facilities and services for the care of children. The state shall take all appropriate measures to ensure that children of working parents have the right to benefit from childcare services and facilities for which they are eligible.

■ Article 20: Children deprived of family environment

Children who are temporarily or permanently deprived by their family have a right to special care and protection and are assisted by the state. The state, in accordance with national laws, will ensure appropriate care for such a child. The child will be found a suitable location in which to be brought up by individuals who respect their ethnic group, religion, culture and language.

■ Article 22: Refugee children

The state will take appropriate measures to ensure that a child who is seeking refugee status or who is considered a refugee by law, whether unaccompanied or accompanied by his or her parents or by any other person, receives appropriate protection and humanitarian assistance in the enjoyment of applicable rights.

If applicable, states shall provide co-operation to protect and assist a child in tracing their parents or other members of the family in order to be reunited. In cases where no parents or other members of the family can be found, the child shall be provided with the same protection as any other child permanently or temporarily deprived of his or her family for any reason.

■ Article 23: Children with disabilities

Children with any kind of disability have the right to enjoy a full life and special care and support, as well the other rights set forth in the convention. The child has a right to access to education, training, healthcare services, rehabilitation services, preparation for employment and recreation opportunities in a manner conducive to the child's achieving the fullest possible social integration and individual development, including his or her cultural and spiritual development.

■ **Article 24: Health and health services**
Children have the right to the best possible healthcare and access to facilities to treat illnesses. The state shall take appropriate measures to:
■ Diminish infant and child mortality
■ Ensure the provision of quality healthcare to all children
- Combat disease and malnutrition through the provision of adequate nutritious foods and clean drinking water
- Consider the dangers and risks of environmental pollution
- Ensure appropriate pre-natal and post-natal healthcare for mothers
- Ensure that everyone in society has access to information on health and nutrition
- Develop preventive healthcare and provide education and guidance to parents.

The state also recognises the needs of developing countries.

■ **Article 25: Review of treatment in care**
Children who are looked after by their local authorities, rather than their parents, have the right to have their living arrangements examined regularly to see if they are the most appropriate setting for the particular child.

■ **Article 26: Social security**
Children, either directly or through their parents or guardians, have the right to help from the state if they are poor or in need.

■ **Article 27: Adequate standard of living**
Children have the right to a standard of living that meets their development, including physical, mental, spiritual, moral and social development. The state should help families and guardians who cannot afford to provide this, particularly with regard to food, clothing and housing.

■ **Article 28: Right to education**
All children have the right to a primary education, which should be free. Different forms of secondary education are encouraged, e.g. vocational education. Wealthy countries should encourage this right in developing countries. Discipline in schools should respect children's dignity and must not involve any physical or mental violence. The state ensures that schools have policies and procedures in place in relation to discipline.

■ **Article 29: Goals of education**

Education should facilitate each child in developing their personality, talents and abilities. It should encourage children to respect others, human rights and their own and other people's cultures. It should also help them learn to live peacefully, protect the environment and respect other people. Children have a particular responsibility to respect the rights of their parents; education should aim to develop respect for the values and culture of parents.

■ **Article 30: Children of minorities/indigenous groups**

Minority or indigenous children have the right to learn about and practise their own culture, language and religion. The right to practise one's own culture, language and religion applies to everyone.

■ **Article 31: Leisure, play and culture**

Children have the right to rest, to play and to participate in activities suitable for their particular age. They have the right to equal opportunities to participate in a wide range of cultural, artistic and other recreational activities.

■ **Article 42: Knowledge of rights**

Governments should make the convention known to adults and children by appropriate means.

Protection

Protection rights include protection from abuse, neglect, exploitation and cruelty, along with the rights to protection from war or abuse in the criminal justice system.

■ **Article 4: Protection of rights**

Governments have a responsibility to take the necessary measures to ensure that children's rights are respected and fulfilled. This involves assessing their social services, legal, health and educational systems, as well as levels of funding for these services. They must help families protect children's rights and create an environment where they can grow and reach their potential. In some instances, this may involve changing existing laws or creating new ones.

■ **Article 11: Kidnapping**

Governments should take the necessary measures to prevent children being taken out of their own country illegally.

■ **Article 19: Protection from all forms of violence**

Children have the right to be protected from any kind of abuse, whether it be physical, mental or sexual abuse, injury, neglect or exploitation while being cared for by their parents, guardians or any other person who is looking after them. The convention does not specify what forms of punishment parents should use; however, any form of discipline involving violence is unacceptable.

When necessary, the state must ensure that effective procedures are in place for the establishment of social programmes to help and support the child. Also necessary are forms of prevention, e.g. follow-up and identification in the case of judicial involvement.

■ Article 20: Children deprived of family environment

Children who are temporarily or permanently deprived by their family have a right to special care and protection and are assisted by the state. The state, in accordance with national laws, will ensure appropriate care for such a child. The child will be found a suitable location in which to be brought up by individuals who respect their ethnic group, religion, culture and language.

■ Article 21: Adoption

Children have the right to care and protection if they are adopted or placed in foster care. This right is the same whether they are adopted in the country where they were born or they are taken to live in another country.

■ Article 22: Refugee children

The state will take appropriate measures to ensure that a child who is seeking refugee status or who is considered a refugee by law, whether unaccompanied or accompanied by his or her parents or by any other person, receives appropriate protection and humanitarian assistance in the enjoyment of applicable rights.

If applicable, states shall provide co-operation to protect and assist a child in tracing their parents or other members of the family in order to be reunited. In cases where no parents or other members of the family can be found, the child shall be provided with the same protection as any other child permanently or temporarily deprived of his or her family for any reason.

■ Article 32: Child labour

The state should protect children from work that exploits them and is dangerous in any way to their health or education. Children's work should not interfere with any of their other rights, including the right to education or the right to relaxation and play. The state will take necessary measures to ensure the implementation of this article and will provide a minimum age that a young person can begin employment, regulate the hours and conditions of such employment and provide appropriate penalties to ensure that this right is protected.

■ **Article 33: Drug abuse**

The state will take appropriate measures, including legislative, administrative, social and educational, to protect children from the use of harmful drugs and from being used in the illicit production and trafficking of drugs.

■ **Article 34: Sexual exploitation**

The state will protect children from all forms of sexual exploitation and abuse. The state will do everything possible to prevent the inducement or coercion of a child to engage in any unlawful sexual activity, the exploitative use of children in prostitution or other unlawful sexual practices or the exploitative use of children in pornographic performances and materials.

■ **Article 35: Abduction, sale and trafficking**

The state should take all measures possible to make sure that children are not abducted, sold or trafficked.

■ **Article 36: Other forms of exploitation**

The state shall protect the child against all other forms of exploitation prejudicial to any aspects of the child's welfare.

■ **Article 37: Detention and punishment**

The state shall ensure that no child is subjected to torture, inhumane or degrading treatment or punishment. Children who break the law should not be treated cruelly. Neither capital punishment nor life imprisonment without the possibility of release is imposed on persons below the age of 18. No child shall be deprived of their liberty. The arrest, detention or imprisonment of a child shall be in conformity with the law and shall be used only as a last resort and for the shortest appropriate period of time. Any child deprived of liberty shall be treated with respect and in a manner which takes into account the needs of their age. They shall be separated from adults unless it is considered in the child's best interests not to do so and shall have the right to maintain contact with his or her family through correspondence and visits. They will have the right to legal and other appropriate assistance as well as the right to challenge the legality of the deprivation of their liberty before the courts.

■ **Article 38: War and armed conflicts**

The state ensures that children under the age of 15 do not take part and are not forced to take part in a war or to join the armed forces. The preferred age of young people joining the armed forces is 18 years of age. The state will take all feasible measures to ensure protection and care of children who are affected by an armed conflict.

■ Article 39: Rehabilitation of child victims

The state will provide children who have been neglected, abused or exploited the necessary help to recover and adapt back into society. Such recovery will take place in an environment which fosters the health, self-respect and dignity of the child.

■ Article 40: Juvenile justice

The state recognises that children who are accused of breaking the law have the right to legal help and fair treatment in a justice system that respects their rights. Every child is presumed innocent until proven guilty. Children are informed promptly of the charge against them, if appropriate through their parents or guardians. The child has the right to legal assistance in the preparation and presentation of their defence. The matter should have a fair hearing according to law, while taking into account the child's age and situation. The child should have free assistance of an interpreter if they cannot speak or understand the language. The child has their privacy protected at all times.

■ Article 41: Respect for superior national standards

If the laws of a particular country provide children with greater protection of their rights than the articles in the convention, those laws should apply.

Participation

Participation rights include the right to express opinions, the right to information and the right to freedom of association. Having these rights in place will help and prepare children to be an active member of society.

■ Article 4: Protection of rights

Governments have a responsibility to take the necessary measures to ensure that children's rights are respected and fulfilled. This involves assessing their social services, legal, health and educational systems, as well as levels of funding for these services. They must help families protect children's rights and create an environment where they can grow and reach their potential. In some instances, this may involve changing existing laws or creating new ones.

■ Article 12: Respect for the views of the child

When adults are making decisions that affect children, a child who is capable of forming their own views has the right to express those views freely. The views of the child should be given due weight, in accordance with the age and maturity of the child. Children have the right to have their opinions taken into account. The child shall in particular be provided the opportunity to be heard in any judicial and administrative proceedings affecting them.

■   **Article 13: Freedom of expression**

Children have the right to freedom of expression, including freedom to seek and receive information through various types of media, provided the information is not damaging to them or the reputations of other people.

■   **Article 14: Freedom of thought, conscience and religion**

The state must respect the right of the child to freedom of thought, conscience and religion. The convention respects the rights and duties of parents in providing religious and moral guidance to their children. Children have the right to examine and practise their religion, as long as they respect other people while doing so. The convention recognises that when children mature they will form their own views; some may question certain religious practices or cultural traditions.

■   **Article 16: Freedom of association**

Children have the right to congregate and join groups and organisations, as long as this does not affect the rights of other people.

■   **Article 16: Right to privacy**

Children have a right to privacy. No child shall be subjected to unlawful interference with their privacy, family, home or correspondence nor unlawful attacks on their honour or reputation.

■   **Article 17: Access to information**

Children have the right to access information relating to their health and wellbeing. Governments should encourage media (radio, television, newspapers and internet sources) to provide information that children can understand and that will not cause them any unnecessary harm. Mass media should particularly be encouraged to supply information in languages that minority and indigenous children can understand. Children should have access to a variety of children's books.

Childcare Act 1991

The Childcare Act 1991 is a very important piece of legislation because it is primarily concerned with the protection and welfare of children. The Act itself is divided up into ten parts, each one dealing with a different aspect of child welfare and protection.

Section 1

This section of the Act provides definitions of various terms used throughout the Act, e.g. it defines a child as anyone under 18, parents as biological or adoptive parents, the health board, health board area, etc.

Section 2

This section of the Act outlines the functions of the health boards in relation to child protection. The health boards (now HSE) have the right to take children whom they believe to be at risk into care; however, they should do so in consultation with the child's parents or guardians. This part of the Act also instructs the health boards to provide care and accommodation to children who are abandoned or homeless. The health boards are also instructed to manage with full parental consent the adoption of children. This is something that the recent Children's Referendum has changed. Parents are no longer able to deny their children the right to be adopted by another family. This section of the Act also set up childcare advisory committees, whose job it is to oversee and review the services being provided by the health boards under the Act. The Act also outlines the health boards' duties in the regulation and support of voluntary bodies providing services to vulnerable children.

Section 3

This section deals with the protection of children in emergencies. The Act states that if it is reported to a member of An Garda Síochána and he/she believes that a child is in immediate danger, they must remove that child to safety. They have no need for a warrant and can break into a house or other dwelling if necessary. The Gardaí then need to alert the health board (HSE), who must then either apply for an emergency care order through the district court (to take the child into care) or return the child to his/her parents if this is deemed safe. This process should take no longer than three days. A justice of the court, on granting an emergency care order, may decide to withhold the location of the child in care from parents or persons *in loco parentis*. The justice may also order a medical or psychiatric examination of the child and may request that they receive treatment without parental consent. The health board (HSE) must then inform the parents or persons *in loco parentis* (if they can be found) that the child has been taken into care. It is the duty of the health board (HSE) to provide suitable accommodation for the child.

Section 4

This section deals with care proceedings regarding children deemed to be requiring care or protection by the state from abuse or neglect (whether or not an emergency care order is in place). Firstly an *interim care order* will be sought. An interim care order allows a child be taken into care for a period of eight days (or longer if a parent or person *in loco parentis* agrees, or if the child is in danger) until a more long-term decision can be made on the case. An application is then made for a *care order*. If the court decides that a child is at risk of being abused or neglected, they will grant the care order. A care order commits the child to the care of the health board (HSE) until they are 18 years of age or for a shorter period if circumstances change (e.g. it is deemed safe for them to return home). While in care, the health board (HSE) has responsibility for the child's health and wellbeing. If a child is deemed to be at risk, but not so much so as to be removed from the care of their parents or person *in loco parentis*, then a *supervision order* may be put in place. A supervision order permits health board (HSE) personnel to visit the child in order to check on their welfare. If a parent or person *in loco parentis* is unhappy with the way the health board is carrying out its duties in this regard, they can have their complaint legally investigated. The health board must follow any direction given by the courts in this regard. Supervision orders last for 12 months (or less if situations improve) and if necessary a new order must be applied for before the old one expires.

Section 5

This section called *Jurisdiction and Procedure* states that in all circumstances the welfare of the child is most important. Having regard to the child's age and understanding, the wishes of the child shall also be considered. Children will have access to a solicitor free of charge and the courts may appoint a *guardian ad litem* for the child. A *guardian ad litem* is someone who acts as an advocate for the child – they will make the child's wishes known to the court and may also liaise with the child's family or with other organisations working with the child, e.g. their school. This section also states that care proceedings must be held in private and that no material can be printed about the case that could lead to the identity of the child being revealed. If a parent or person *in loco parentis* refuses to deliver up a child to the court, they may be physically forced to do so.

Section 6

This section describes the types of care options that may be available to a child. These include with a foster parent, within a residential unit or with a potential adoptive parent. Sometimes children are placed with family friends or relatives if this is deemed satisfactory by the health board (HSE). The health board is also responsible for arranging safe and suitable access to children in care by their parents or persons *in loco parentis* or other people deemed by the health board to have a bona fide interest in the child. If parents believe that access arrangements are unsatisfactory, they may apply to the courts for it to be reviewed. In the interests of the child's safety, a court order may exist that prohibits a named person from having access to the child. This section of the Act also requires the government minister responsible for children in care to compile a list of regulations for residential care units, foster parents and relatives caring for children and to monitor compliance with them. If placements are deemed unsatisfactory for any reason, children can be removed. This section of the Act requires the health board to provide aftercare support for children leaving care, up until they are 21 years of age (or older if they are still in full-time education). The Act outlines what this aftercare should include.

Section 7

This section of the Act deals with *Supervision of Pre-School Services* and it led directly to the compilation of the Child Care (Pre-School) Regulations 2006.

Section 8

This section of the Act deals with Children's Residential Centres. Such centres must register with the health board (HSE) and must comply with regulations pertaining to such centres. Centres failing to comply with the regulations may be removed from the register and prohibited from operating as a children's residential centre.

Sections 9 and 10

These sections deal with a number of administrative issues including the compilation of regulations on foot of the Act, the powers of the minister for health with regards to this Act and the functions of the health board CEO with regards to this Act. Section 10 details amendments to older pieces of legislation that this Act will require, i.e. amendments to the School Attendance Act 1926 and the Guardianship of Infants Act 1964.

Child Care (Pre-School) Regulations 2006

Child Care (Pre-School Services) (No 2) Regulations 2006 was produced by the Department of Health and Children, on foot of the Childcare Act 1991. The regulations came into effect in 2007 and they are concerned with much more than early childhood curriculum provision alone. The regulations outline the legal requirements a pre-school service is obliged to meet.

The regulations cover many areas, including:

- Health, welfare and development of the child
- First aid
- Medical assistance
- Management and staffing
- Behaviour management
- Notice to be given by persons proposing to carry out a pre-school service
- Notification of change in circumstances

- Number of pre-school children who may be catered for
- Register of pre-school children
- Records
- Information for parents
- Fire safety measures
- Premises and facilities
  - Heating
  - Ventilation
  - Lighting
  - Sanitary accommodation
  - Drainage and sewage disposal
  - Waste storage and disposal
  - Equipment and materials
  - Food and drink
  - Safety measures
  - Facilities for rest and play
- Furnishing of information to the HSE
- Insurance
- Annual fees
- Inspection
- Enforcement and execution.

These regulations have major significance for the quality of early childhood curriculum provision. All pre-school facilities are now legally obliged to have certain clearly defined requirements in place and all facilities are subject to inspection by officers of the Health Service Executive (HSE) to ensure that requirements are met. While compliance with the regulations has meant considerable amounts of extra work and expense on service providers, it has also resulted in a more uniform standard of service across the sector. Once this basic standard of service exists, then it is possible for more targeted initiatives to be realised, e.g. Síolta and Aistear.

A complete copy of the regulations can be found at http://www.childcareonline.ie/files/ 1239967888.pdf.

Parental Leave Acts 1998 and 2006

The 1998 Act came into operation on 3 December 1998 and was amended in 2006. This Act entitles a natural or adoptive parent of a child to take 14 weeks' unpaid leave from their job in order to care for their child. Parental leave can be taken as a fourteen-week block or with the consent of the employer in smaller amounts, e.g. one or more days per week, or one or more hours per day, over a period of time totalling no more than 14 weeks.

Parents can take leave in respect of a birth child up until the child is eight years old. In the case of a child adopted aged 6–8, leave can be taken for two years after the date of the adoption order. In the case of a child with special needs, leave can be taken up until the child is 16 years old.

Employees with more than one child can only take one fourteen-week block of leave in any twelve-month period, unless their children are multiples (i.e. twins or triplets). Each parent is entitled to this leave, but one parent cannot transfer their leave to the other unless they work for the same employer and their employer agrees to this arrangement. If a parent becomes unwell on parental leave and is unable to care for their child, parental leave will be suspended until after the illness.

While on parental leave, you must be regarded (for employment rights purposes) as still working. This means that you can build up annual leave while on parental leave. If your annual holidays are due during parental leave, they may be taken at a later time. A public holiday that falls while you are on parental leave and on a day when you would normally be working is added to your period of leave. Generally, you must be working with your employer for at least one year before applying for parental leave.

Children First: National Guidance for the Protection and Welfare of Children (2011)

Children First: National Guidance for the Protection and Welfare of Children was published by the Department of Children and Youth Affairs in 2011. This edition of the guidelines supersedes all previous editions, e.g. *Children First* (1999), and it should be the only edition used by people working with children. The principal piece of legislation underpinning the guidelines is the Childcare Act 1991 (see p.29).

One of the main points of the Children First guidelines is that *everyone* has a duty to protect children and that this is not simply the job of the Gardaí, social workers or other health professionals. For this reason, everyone working with children and young people should be very aware of the contents of the Children First guidelines and, if possible, avail of child protection training. A complete copy of the Children First guidelines can be downloaded at http://www.dcya.gov.ie/documents/child_welfare_protection/ChildrenFirst.pdf.

Structure of the Guidelines

The guidance document is divided into four parts, which are subdivided into chapters as follows.
- Part I
  - Principles, Aims and Use of *Children First: National Guidance*
- Part II
  - Definition and Recognition of Child Abuse
  - Basis for reporting concerns and Standard Reporting Procedure
- Interagency Co-operation: Roles and responsibilities of organisations and personnel working with children
- Part III
  - Assessment and Management of child protection and welfare concerns
  - Supervision, Support and Additional Guidance for HSE child protection and welfare work
  - Protocol for An Garda Síochána–HSE Liaison
- Part IV
  - Especially vulnerable children
  - Peer abuse
  - Training in child protection and welfare.

A summary of certain sections is provided here but it is best if students download and read a copy of the guidelines in full.

Part I

Principles of the Guidelines

Towards the beginning of the guidelines, ten key principles that should inform best practice in child protection and welfare are given. These principles are very important and they underpin everything else in the guidelines.

1. The welfare of children is of paramount importance.
2. Early intervention and support should be available to promote the welfare of children and families, particularly where they are vulnerable or at risk of not receiving adequate care or protection. Family support should form the basis of early intervention and preventative interventions.
3. A proper balance must be struck between protecting children and respecting the rights and needs of parents/carers and families. Where there is conflict, the child's welfare must come first.
4. Children have a right to be heard, listened to and taken seriously. Taking account of their age and understanding, they should be consulted and involved in all matters and decisions that may affect their lives. Where there are concerns about a child's welfare, there should be opportunities provided for their views to be heard independently of their parents/carers.
5. Parents/carers have a right to respect and should be consulted and involved in matters that concern their family.
6. Factors such as the child's family circumstances, gender, age, stage of development, religion, culture and race should be considered when taking protective action. Intervention should not deal with the child in isolation; the child's circumstances must be understood within a family context.
7. The criminal dimension of any action must not be ignored.
8. Children should only be separated from parents/carers when alternative means of protecting them have been exhausted. Re-union should be considered in the context of planning for the child's future.
9. The prevention, detection and treatment of child abuse or neglect requires a co-ordinated multi-disciplinary approach, effective management, clarity of responsibility and training of personnel in organisations working with children.
10. Professionals and agencies working with adults who for a range of reasons may have serious difficulties meeting their children's basic needs for safety and security should always consider the impact of their adult client/patient's behaviour on a child and act in the child's best interests.

Aims of the Guidelines

The guidelines are intended to assist people in identifying and reporting concerns related to child abuse and neglect. The roles and responsibilities of the HSE and An Garda Síochána are highlighted, as are the importance of interagency co-operation and multi-disciplinary responses. The guidelines also highlight the importance of training, supervision and support services for children and their families.

Use of the Guidelines

Use of the guidelines will help to ensure best practice in the recruitment of staff or volunteers: Garda vetting, taking up of references, good HR practices in interviewing, induction training, probation and ongoing supervision and management. The guidelines also help to ensure that staff members or volunteers can recognise signs of child abuse or neglect and that they know what to do if they have reasonable grounds for concern. All organisations must identify a designated person to act as a liaison with outside agencies if a child protection issue arises within their organisation. The designated person is responsible for reporting allegations or suspicions of child abuse to the HSE Children and Family Services or to An Garda Síochána.

Part II

Definitions of Child Abuse

This chapter of the guidelines (along with its appendices) describes the four principal types of child abuse – neglect, emotional abuse, physical abuse and sexual abuse – and offers guidance on how to recognise such abuse. A child may be subjected to one or more forms of abuse at any given time. The guidelines offer a definition of the child as a person under the age of 18.

Neglect

Neglect can be defined in terms of an omission, where the child suffers significant harm or impairment of development by being deprived of food, clothing, warmth, hygiene, intellectual stimulation, supervision and safety, attachment to and affection from adults, and/or medical care. Neglect generally occurs over a period of time rather than at one specific point in time. For example, a child whose mother is going into hospital to have another baby might be fed junk food for the day. Since this is a once-off incident, it is not considered neglect. However, children who are fed junk food all the time may be considered to be neglected in this regard.

Emotional Abuse

Emotional abuse is normally a feature of the *relationship* between a parent/carer and a child rather than in a specific event or pattern of events. It occurs when a child's developmental needs for affection, approval, consistency and security are not met. Children who are constantly criticised, blamed, given too much responsibility, over- or under-protected, ignored or given no affection are considered to be emotionally abused. Children may be abused in other ways at the same time. If emotional abuse occurs by itself, it can be very difficult to recognise unless it is witnessed directly.

Physical Abuse

Physical abuse results in actual or potential physical harm from an action or lack of action that is reasonably within the control of a parent/carer. There may be single or repeated incidents. Physical abuse includes imposition of severe physical punishment; beating, slapping, hitting or kicking; pushing, shaking or throwing; pinching, biting, choking or hair-pulling; terrorising with threats; observing violence; use of excessive force in handling; deliberate poisoning, e.g. with alcohol or medication; suffocation; fabricated/induced illness; allowing or creating a substantial risk of significant harm to a child.

Sexual Abuse

Sexual abuse occurs when a child is used by another person for his or her gratification or sexual arousal, or for that of others. Examples include: exposure of the sexual organs or any sexual act intentionally performed in the presence of a child; intentional touching or molesting of the body of a child; masturbation in the presence of a child or the involvement of the child in an act of masturbation; sexual intercourse with a child, whether oral, vaginal or anal; sexual exploitation of a child, e.g. prostitution or pornography; and consensual sexual activity involving an adult and an underage person (a boy or girl under 17 years).

Recognition of Child Abuse

Child neglect or abuse can often be difficult to identify and may present in many forms. A list of indicators of child neglect and abuse is contained in Appendix 1 of the Children First guidelines. Because of its importance to childcare practitioners, this list of indicators is given in full in Appendix 1 of this book (see p.182). It must be stressed that usually no single indicator can be seen as conclusive evidence of abuse, since it may indicate conditions other than child abuse. All signs and symptoms must be examined in the broader context of the child's situation and their family circumstances.

The ability to recognise child abuse can depend as much on a person's willingness to accept the possibility of its existence as their actual knowledge and information. There are usually three stages in the identification of child abuse: (1) considering the possibility of abuse, (2) looking out for signs of abuse and (3) recording of information.

Basis for Reporting Concerns

Everyone must be alert to the possibility that children with whom they are in contact may be suffering from abuse or neglect. This responsibility is particularly relevant for professionals such as teachers, childcare professionals, health professionals and those working with adults with serious parenting difficulties. It is also an important responsibility for staff and people involved in sports clubs, community activities, youth clubs, the religious sector and other organisations catering for children.

HSE Child and Family Services must be informed if a person has a *reasonable concern* that a child is or may be at risk of being abused or neglected. A concern about a potential risk to children posed by a specific person, even if the children are unidentifiable, should also be communicated to the HSE Children and Family Services. Anonymity cannot be guaranteed to persons reporting abuse, especially when information is sought as part of legal proceedings.

Designated Liaison Persons

Every organisation (both public and private) providing services for children should identify a *designated child protection liaison person* to act as a liaison with outside agencies and as a resource person for staff. He/she is responsible for ensuring that the standard reporting procedure is followed, so that suspected cases of child neglect or abuse are referred promptly to the designated person in the HSE Children and Family Services or, in the event of an emergency and the unavailability of the HSE, to An Garda Síochána. He/she should be knowledgeable about child protection and should undertake regular training to remain up to date.

Standard Reporting Procedure

Any person reporting a child abuse/neglect concern should do so without delay to the HSE Children and Family Services. Reports can be made in person, by telephone or in writing. Contact numbers for HSE offices nationwide can be obtained in Appendix 2 of the Children First guidelines, online (www.hse.ie/go/socialworkers) or by phoning LoCall 1850 241 850.

Before deciding whether or not to make a formal report, you may wish to discuss your concerns with a health professional or directly with the HSE Children and Family Services but *under no circumstances should a child be left in a situation that exposes them to harm or to risk of harm pending HSE intervention.* In the event of an emergency where you think a child is in immediate danger and you cannot get in contact with the HSE, you should contact the Gardaí. This may be done through any Garda station. A copy of the Standard Reporting Form is given in Appendix 2 of this book (see p.187). It is worth noting that the HSE must follow up on referrals whether or not the standard reporting form has been used.

Relevant Legislation

Protections for Persons Reporting Child Abuse Act 1998 makes provision for the protection from civil liability of persons who have reported child abuse 'reasonably and in good faith' to designated officers of the HSE or to any member of An Garda Síochána. This protection applies to organisations as well as to individuals. This means that even if a communicated suspicion of child abuse proves unfounded it would have to be proven that the person/organisation had not acted reasonably and in good faith in making the report.

The Data Protection Acts 1998 and 2003 and The Freedom of Information Acts 1997 and 2003 are also relevant to child protection.

Interagency Co-operation/Roles and Responsibilities

This section outlines the roles of different personnel working specifically within the area of child protection and also with children generally. It is important for childcare practitioners to have a good understanding of these roles and of the concept of interagency co-operation.

Interagency Co-operation

No one professional has all the skills, knowledge or resources necessary to comprehensively meet all the requirements of an individual child protection case. Therefore, it is essential that all professionals and organisations involved with a child and his or her parents/carers work together to deliver a co-ordinated and comprehensive response.

Roles and Responsibilities of the HSE Children and Family Services

Under the Child Care Act 1991, the HSE has certain statutory obligations for the protection and welfare of children.

1. The HSE must be open to receiving information from any source about a child who may not be receiving adequate care and protection.
2. Having received such information, the HSE must seek to establish whether the child in question is receiving adequate care and protection. It must co-ordinate information from all relevant sources and make an assessment of the situation.
3. Having identified a child who is not receiving adequate care and protection, the HSE is under a duty to take appropriate action to promote the welfare of the child.

Roles and Responsibilities of An Garda Síochána

An Garda Síochána have three primary roles in relation to child protection. They must:

- Thoroughly investigate cases of alleged child abuse and/or neglect and bring offenders to justice
- Intervene with HSE personnel (or alone where HSE personnel are not on duty) to protect a child or children in immediate risk of harm or abuse
- Provide vetting, through the Garda Central Vetting Unit (GCVU), on behalf of organisations employing personnel to work in a full-time, part-time, voluntary or student placement capacity with children and/or vulnerable adults.

Roles and Responsibilities of Other Health Sector Personnel

While there are HSE personnel specifically employed to work within the area of child protection, many others also have important roles to play. This section of the guidelines provides detail on the roles of general practitioners (GPs), primary care teams, public health nurses, hospitals, mental health and addiction services and child and adolescent psychiatric services. While each of these services will have their own areas of expertise and skill, together they have a responsibility while working with children to use this expertise and skill to (1) consider the possibility of abuse, (2) look out for signs and (3) record information.

Roles and Responsibilities of other Organisations Working with Children

In this section, the guidelines refer to all organisations that work with and care for children, including: schools; private companies, e.g. crèches; voluntary organisations, e.g. football clubs; and charities. Some specific guidance is given for particular sectors (e.g. schools) but generally all organisations must:

■ Provide clear guidance for staff, volunteers and students on work placement in relation to child protection

■ Appoint a designated person within the organisation with specific responsibility for child protection

■ Ensure that all personnel are Garda vetted before beginning work within the organisation.

For a detailed account of all of these roles and responsibilities, see pp.18–27 of *Children First*.

Guidance for HSE Children and Family Services and Other Professionals

This section offers guidance on the steps to be taken by staff in the HSE Children and Family Services and other professionals in responding to reported child protection and welfare concerns. It describes the assessment process to be followed in establishing whether reasonable grounds for concern exist and it gives guidance on the effective use of child protection conferences, the development of a child protection plan and protection review conferences.

While some of the detail in this section of the guidelines is not of direct relevance to childcare practitioners, it is good for all individuals working with children to have an understanding of what happens after a child protection concern is raised with HSE Children and Family Services. A summary of the process is provided below.

■ If a child protection concern has been raised with the HSE Children and Family Services it will be followed up without delay by an appointed social worker. The social worker will notify the child/children's parents or guardians that a child protection concern has been raised unless by doing so would put the child/children further at risk. The Gardaí may also be informed at this stage.

■ The social worker will then begin preliminary screening and enquiries. He/she will find out if the case is already known to the HSE and if it is will contact the people previously involved and establish what is already known.

■ An initial assessment will then be carried out. This assessment may involve: talking to the child and his or her parents/carers to help establish whether grounds for concern exist; a medical examination and treatment; talking to other people involved with the child, e.g. a GP or teacher, to identify the nature and severity of any risks; identifying any strengths and protective factors that appear to lessen the risk, e.g. supportive extended family.

■ If a decision is made to offer services to a child and his or her parents/carers, a key worker will be allocated to the case and a decision will be made on initial protective action to be taken. Usually a family support plan and a child welfare plan will be compiled.

■ If concerns are considered to be *unfounded*, (1) this must be stated in the case file, (2) Gardaí must be informed and (3) the child and family must be supported, e.g. with counselling.

■ *Family support plans* aim to support families whose children's welfare is under threat. Supports take a variety of forms and are designed to prevent children having to enter the care system. (Sometimes, however, child protection issues are such that children cannot remain with their families and must be taken into the care system.) If a family is receiving family support, their needs will be identified and supports targeted accordingly. For example, if children were being neglected due to parental alcohol misuse, family support would involve linking with addiction services. Families are encouraged to identify their own solutions as much as possible.

■ *Child welfare plans* incorporate family support plans (above) and also actions specific to the child. Both family support plans and child welfare plans are reviewed and evaluated regularly and thoroughly and if they are considered to be unsuccessful a *child protection conference* will be held. This meeting is normally organised and chaired by a HSE social work manager and will involve all the relevant agencies working with the child and their family, e.g. An Garda Síochána, crèche, pre-schools, addiction services, etc. The child's parents/carers will also be present unless doing so would not be in the child's best interests. Agencies may be asked to be present for only part of the conference.

■ During the conference an interagency *child protection plan* will be formulated. The plan will identify current and potential risks to the child. It will identify strategies to protect the child, identify who is responsible for implementation of named strategies and identify the resources needed to carry out the plan. The conference will consult with the child and his or her parents/carers (if applicable) on the content and feasibility of the plan and also set a date for a review of the plan. The child's name will be entered on the Child Protection Notification System (CPNS).

■ When a child protection plan has been put in place, it is the responsibility of all identified professionals and agencies to implement those parts of the plan that relate to them and to communicate with the key worker.

■ The role of the key worker is to distribute the plan to all involved, explain key aspects of the plan to the child and if applicable his/her family. Key workers should give families a list of all personnel involved in the plan and inform them of any change in personnel.

■ A child protection *review* conference will be held six months after the child protection conference (or sooner if appropriate). All agencies involved with the child and their family will normally be asked to submit a written report regarding the case. Progress on the case will be evaluated and further actions planned where necessary. Sometimes no further actions are necessary and the review may ask for the delisting of the child's name from the Child Protection Notification System.

Emergency Action to Protect a Child

If a report made to the HSE Children and Family Services indicates the presence of immediate and serious risk, urgent action must be taken to protect any children in that situation who may be in danger. This may involve securing the co-operation of a protective carer, family member or other responsible adult in the child's home whose capacity to protect the child can be defined and agreed. If this is not possible the child may need to be placed in the care of the HSE, preferably with the consent of the parents/carers but if necessary using legal measures under the Child Care Act 1991. Removal of children from their homes is very stressful and requires sensitive handling. The likely effects of separation must be balanced against the danger of leaving the child at home.

If there is reason to believe that a medical examination will indicate more clearly whether or not a child has been physically abused or seriously deprived or neglected, or if a child appears to require medical treatment, then a doctor with appropriate experience should carry out the examination in consultation with An Garda Síochána. If there is reason to believe that a specialist assessment will indicate more clearly whether a child has been sexually abused, a referral should be made to the child sexual abuse assessment service for the area where a doctor with appropriate training and experience should carry out a physical examination for sexual abuse. Parents/carers should be asked for permission and given the opportunity to attend. If permission is refused, parents/carers should be informed of the HSE's option to apply for an emergency care order or supervision order.

Case Transfers and Serious Incident Reviews

The HSE Children and Family Services should have a *case transfer protocol* in place. This protocol explains what must be done if a child about whom there are protection or welfare concerns and/or his or her parents/carers move to another jurisdiction or to another area within the HSE.

Serious incident reviews occur after a serious incident, e.g. a child dies in care or a child dies who is known to the HSE child protection system. The review closely evaluates the circumstances surrounding the serious incident and in this way tries to identify possible deficits in the system.

The remainder of this section of the guidelines deals with the following issues: HSE record keeping, supervision and support of HSE child protection staff, guidance on interviewing parents/carers and children, and dealing with conflict between children and their parent/carers. Since these aspects are not directly relevant to the work of childcare professionals, they will not be explored here. However, they can be read on pp.41–5 of *Children First*.

Protocol for An Garda Síochána–HSE Liaison

This section of the guidelines provides detailed information for members of An Garda Síochána involved with child protection cases. While certain details of the guidelines are not required by childcare professionals, it is useful to have a broad overview of how a child protection case progresses, the personnel involved and their roles.

The HSE and An Garda Síochána are the two principal agencies empowered by law to carry out assessments and investigations of suspected child abuse and neglect. An Garda Síochána has the additional responsibility of preparing an investigation file for the Director of Public Prosecutions (DPP), who decides on and carries out prosecutions. An Garda Síochána has the power to remove a child to safety under Section 12 of the Child Care Act 1991 if there are reasonable grounds for believing that there is an immediate and serious risk to the child. The child shall be delivered into the custody of the HSE as soon as possible. As with the HSE, a member of the Gardaí will be appointed as the officer designated to a particular case.

Cases to be Formally Notified by the HSE to An Garda Síochána and Vice Versa

Where the HSE suspects that a child is being physically or sexually abused or wilfully neglected, they are obliged to formally inform the local Garda Superintendent using the Standard Notification Form. If a criminal prosecution is not expected (e.g. unintentional neglect) the Gardaí do not have to be informed. Where doubt exists, however, the Gardaí should be consulted for advice. The Garda Superintendent appoints a Garda and designates him/her to the case. Without delay this Garda must make contact with the HSE social worker connected with the case. They begin working on the case by completing the Record of Garda–HSE Liaison Form. At the same time, the Superintendent appoints an inspector/sergeant to manage the investigation of the case.

The same process must occur where An Garda Síochána suspects that a child is being physically or sexually abused or wilfully neglected. This must be done without delay and the Gardaí do not have to have sufficient evidence to support a criminal prosecution before notifying the HSE.

Part IV

This section of the guidelines provides additional information on three very important issues relating to child protection:

◼ Vulnerable children
◼ Peer abuse
◼ Training in child protection and welfare.

Vulnerable Children

Although it is possible for any child to be abused or neglected there are children who may be especially vulnerable. These include:

◼ Children in residential settings
◼ Children in the care of the state under the Child Care Act 1991 (foster care, relative care and residential care)
◼ Children who are homeless
◼ Children with disabilities
◼ Separated children seeking asylum
◼ Children being trafficked.

The Social Services Inspectorate (SSI) section of the Health Information and Quality Authority (HIQA) has statutory responsibility (under the Health Act 2007) for inspecting HSE children's residential centres, special care, hostels, relative/foster care and children detention schools. All those caring for children in these settings must be alert to the possibility of abuse by other children, visitors and members of staff. Policies and procedures aimed at preventing abuse must be in place. There must be clear written procedures on how to deal with suspected abuse and these must be accessible and fully explained to children and to staff.

Research has shown that children with disabilities are at an increased risk of abuse. The abuser is most likely to be known to the victim. It is therefore vital that parents, teachers and all staff in services for children with disabilities are familiar with the indicators of abuse and are alert to signs of abuse (see Appendix 1, p.182). All organisations working with children with disabilities should have clear guidelines for preventing, identifying and reporting child abuse or neglect and should ensure that all staff and volunteers are Garda Vetted and trained in the use of the Children First guidelines.

Another vulnerable group of children are those children who are living in Ireland having been separated from their birth parents and whose first language is not English. There are also many children in Ireland who have been trafficked for the purposes of exploitation (sexual exploitation or child labour). Sometimes through fear these children resist HSE intervention.

Homeless children regularly come to the attention of the HSE. It is the responsibility of the HSE to work with these young people to investigate why this situation has arisen and to work towards a solution. This may involve medical or psychological supports in addition to the provision of suitable accommodation. The HSE may try to find accommodation for the young person with a suitable relative or, failing that, may arrange to have them placed in a residential unit or in foster care.

Peer Abuse

With some cases of child abuse, the alleged perpetrator will be another child. When this arises it is particularly important to consider how the HSE Children and Family Services and other agencies can provide care for both the child victim and the child abuser. This is particularly important because it has been documented that many adult abusers began abusing as children and many were abused as children themselves.

Sexual Abuse

Peer abuse normally takes one of four forms:

- **Normal sexual exploration**

  This could consist of naive play between two children that involves the exploration of their sexuality. One of the most important aspects of this behaviour is its tone. There should be no coercive or dominating aspects to it. There is usually no need for a child protection intervention in such cases.

- **Abuse reactive behaviour**

  This occurs when a child who has been abused acts out this abuse behaviour on another child. Both children need to be supported by child protection interventions.

- **Sexually obsessive behaviour**

  Children may engage in sexually compulsive behaviour, e.g. excessive masturbation. Not every child who engages in such behaviour has been sexually abused but they may be using this behaviour as a comfort because of other unmet needs, usually emotional needs. These children need specialist help in addressing their unmet needs.

- **Abusive behaviour by adolescents and young people**

  Behaviour that is abusive will have elements of domination, coercion or bribery, and secrecy. Often there is inequality between victim and abuser, e.g. size, age or intellect. Both children should be supported by child protection interventions.

Bullying

> Bullying can be defined as repeated aggression – whether it be verbal, psychological or physical – that is conducted by an individual or group against others. It is behaviour that is intentionally aggravating and intimidating, and occurs mainly among children in social environments such as schools. It includes behaviours such as teasing, taunting, threatening, hitting or extortion by one or more persons against a victim. Bullying can also take the form of racial abuse. With developments in modern technology, children can also be the victims of non-contact bullying, via mobile phones, the internet and other personal devices. (DYCA: 61)

All organisations working with children should have a well-planned policy and set of procedural guidelines for dealing with bullying. Serious incidents of bullying behaviour are child abuse and should be referred to the HSE Children and Family Services.

Training in Child Protection and Welfare

All agencies involved with children have a responsibility to ensure that training in child protection and welfare is available on an ongoing basis. The level and type of training required depends on an individual's role within an organisation. All staff working with children should be trained in the recognition of signs of abuse (see Appendix 1, p.182) and in the procedures that must be followed once there is a suspicion of abuse.

The HSE divides training into two levels: basic and advanced. For most childcare practitioners the basic level of training is sufficient for their work. Basic-level training gives personnel knowledge of the relevant childcare legislation and a working knowledge of policies, procedures and protocols for child protection. The designated child protection liaison person within an organisation would certainly require more advanced training. *Children First* emphasises the need for inter- and intra-agency training, i.e. agencies working together. This type of training is essential since so many failures of child protection have been the result of a breakdown in communication within or between organisations.

Our Duty to Care: The Principles of Good Practice for the Protection of Children and Young People (2002)

This document was published by the Department of Health and Children in 2002 for use by community and voluntary organisations working with children. It offers guidance on the promotion of child welfare and the development of safe practices in work with children. It also gives information on how to recognise signs of child abuse and the correct steps to take within organisations if it is suspected, witnessed or disclosed. *Our Duty to Care* should be used in conjunction with the Children First guidelines and any locally devised guidelines. *Our Duty to Care* has been adapted from the Northern Ireland document of the same name, reflecting a whole-island approach to child protection. The document itself is broken into eight different sections, each dealing with a different aspect of child welfare and protection. In addition to this, the document has eight appendices supplying forms that organisations may find useful (e.g. sample volunteer reference form).

Section 1: Principles of Good Practice

Section 1 of the document outlines the principles of good practice in relation to child welfare and protection. These are very like the principles for best practice in the Children First guidelines (see p.37).

Section 2: Protecting and Promoting Children's Rights

Section 2 demonstrates the ways in which children's rights can be protected and promoted. Organisations can promote children's rights and welfare in lots of ways. They can create an environment in which children are valued, encouraged and affirmed, have their rights respected and are treated as individuals. They can ensure that children know their rights and responsibilities. They can eliminate as far as possible any threatening, violent or degrading behaviour and they can adopt a child protection policy to keep children as safe as possible. One other important way to promote children's rights is to appoint a designated person with overall responsibility for child welfare and protection. This person should be knowledgeable about child welfare and protection, acting as a source of information for staff in the organisation and also knowing how to act if a child welfare or protection issue arises.

This section also explains ways in which other staff members can promote children's rights and wellbeing. Suggestions include listening to children, treating them with dignity and respect, making sure all children are aware of expected behaviour in the setting, asking for their opinions, being fair and consistent, encouraging children to express feelings or fears, knowing the organisation's principles and practices regarding child welfare and protection and responding to allegations. The last part of this section gives indicators to organisations regarding how to establish a code of behaviour between workers and children using the service.

■ While physically comforting a child can be reassuring for the child, it should only take place when all persons concerned are comfortable with it.

- Workers should never physically punish or be in any way verbally abusive to a child, nor should they tell jokes of a sexual nature in the presence of children.
- Workers should be careful not to develop 'favourites' or spend too much time with any one child.
- Children should be encouraged to report cases of bullying to an adult in the setting.
- Workers, as a rule, should not give lifts to children on their own.

Section 3: Recruitment Practices

Section 3 is concerned with the development of safe recruitment practices. While it is acknowledged that the vast majority of people working in community and voluntary organisations are very suited to working there, it is also acknowledged by these guidelines that people with a tendency to abuse children can be attracted to the type of work that gives them the opportunity to be with children. This must always be borne in mind when recruiting new workers. It must be emphasised that recruitment practices must apply to *everyone*. New applicants must be given a clear job description. They should be asked to fill out an application form. They should be asked to sign a declaration stating that there is no reason why they are not suitable for the position. They should be interviewed and they should be asked for references. The references should be checked and the applicants should be asked for ID.

Something that was missing from this document (which has since come into force) is the requirement for Garda clearance before commencement of employment – see *Children First*.

Section 4: Management Procedures and Practices

Section 4 is concerned with the development of safe management procedures and practices. Management should (1) know the children involved with the organisation, (2) keep records (e.g. attendance, accident reports, consent forms or grievances) and (3) know the workers. Managers need to pay attention to ordinary health and safety measures, e.g. fire, first aid and insurance cover. Management should also ensure adequate supervision of children at all times. Overnight trips need particular attention: consent forms, information about children on the trip (e.g. medical problems), appropriate supervision of sleeping arrangements, etc.

With regards to the management of challenging behaviour, management need to have clear policics in place. There must be clear rules and boundaries. Threats or coercion cannot be used. Members of staff do not deal with more serious incidences alone and records of incidents are kept. Staff should be given induction training in these matters and ongoing staff supervision is advised if workers are dealing with challenging issues on an ongoing basis, e.g. a youth club catering for young offenders.

Section 5: Raising Awareness about Child Abuse

This section advises organisations on how to ensure that all of their staff:
- Are clear about what abuse is
- Know how to recognise and respond to it
- Are aware of who can abuse children
- Know what steps to take to report suspected abuse.

This section follows very closely the Children First guidelines and suggests that these should also be referred to for a full account of the four points above.

Section 6: Responding to Accidents and Complaints or to Alleged or Suspected Child Abuse

In dealing with accidents, Section 6 states the following.
- Emergency numbers must be prominently displayed.
- Everyone knows where the nearest phone is located.
- Someone has knowledge and/or training to deal with foreseeable medical and accidental incidents.
- A first aid box is kept where it is easy to find.
- Incident/report forms are available.
- There is a formal complaints procedure for children and parents.
- Workers know what information will be needed.

In terms of dealing with complaints regarding alleged or suspected child abuse, this document reiterates instructions given in the Children First guidelines.

Section 7: Action to be taken when an Allegation is Made Against a Worker Within the Organisation

This section, like the Children First guidelines, outlines the procedures for:
- Reporting the allegation
- Dealing with the worker.

Although the same information is being conveyed in both documents, this document's wording is more accessible than that of Children First and may for this reason be more usable by organisations.

Section 8: Making Links

Section 8 describes how organisations can make links by:

■ Working to involve parents in the organisation
■ Co-operating with other agencies if a child protection concern has arisen
■ Networking to achieve better practice.

The document describes very practical ways in which each of the above may be achieved.

Appendices

Our Duty to Care also contains a total of eight *appendices*, each of which contains details of procedures and forms that will be of great use to community or voluntary organisations. The appendices are as follows.

■ **Appendix 1: Standard reporting procedure**
This is similar to the Children First guidelines.

■ **Appendix 2: Reporting allegations or suspicions of abuse**
There is a suggested template for the reporting of child protection and welfare concerns to a health board (HSE). In cases of emergency (or outside health board hours), reports should be made directly to An Garda Síochána.

■ **Appendix 3: Health boards and An Garda Síochána child protection policies**
This appendix outlines briefly what health board and Garda child protection policies are. Much more detail is provided in the Children First guidelines, but this is nevertheless a useful synopsis.

■ **Appendix 4: Addresses of health board child care managers**
This provides very useful practical information for organisations working with children. This appendix gives the address, fax and phone number of childcare managers in all health board (HSE) areas. If the document was more up-to-date, e-mail addresses would also be included. Nevertheless, this appendix provides a comprehensive list of contact numbers should a child welfare or protection issue arise for an organisation.

■ **Appendix 5: Sample volunteer application form**

■ **Appendix 6: Sample volunteer declaration form**

■ **Appendix 7: Sample volunteer reference form**

■ **Appendix 8: Standard form for reporting child protection and/or welfare concerns**
Note: Some of these appendices have been updated in *Children First* (2011).

Education for Persons with Special Educational Needs Act (EPSEN) 2004

This is the most significant piece of legislation relating to special needs in education. It was intended to be fully implemented by January 2009, but recent budgetary cutbacks have delayed this. The Act comes from the standpoint of inclusion. The Act is very extensive and covers many different areas:

- The issue of inclusion with regards to children with special needs in mainstream settings
- Service provision for children with special educational needs
- Assessment of special needs
- Preparation of individual education plans for children with special needs by educational establishments
- Appeals.

Inclusion

The Act states that:

> A child with special educational needs shall be educated in an inclusive environment with children who do not have such needs unless the nature or degree of those needs of the child is such that to do so would be inconsistent with:

> (*a*) the best interests of the child as determined in accordance with any assessment carried out under this Act,
> **or**
> (*b*) the effective provision of education for children with whom the child is to be educated.

Service Provision and Assessment of Needs

Under section 3 of the Act, if the principal of a school believes that a child with special needs is not making satisfactory progress in the school, they are required to make changes in an attempt to better address the child's needs. Should no progress still be made, the principal must under the Act arrange in consultation with the child's parents an assessment to be carried out with the child within one month through the National Council for Special Education (NCSE).

Individual Education Plan (IEP)

After assessment, the NCSE must prepare an individual education plan (IEP) for the child. An organiser called a Special Education Needs Organiser (SENO) helps to co-ordinate the formation of the plan and the school's implementation of it. Depending on the child and their needs, many people may be involved in the formation of the plan: parents, principal, psychologists, speech and language therapists, physiotherapists, child psychiatrists and occupational therapists. There is, therefore, a crossover between government departments (health and education) here.

Should the principal consider that the individual education plan compiled by the NCSE is unworkable, they can request through the SENO that a revised plan be compiled. Parents can also appeal plans created for their child, e.g. if they feel that the plan does not adequately cater for their child's needs (perhaps they feel their child should have an SNA and this was not granted).

Parents of children younger than school-going age, who suspect their child may have special needs can arrange for assessment through the Health Service Executive (HSE). An individual education plan according to the Act (section 9) must include information on the following:

(a) the nature and degree of the child's abilities, skills and talents
(b) the nature and degree of the child's special educational needs and how those needs affect his or her educational development
(c) the present level of educational performance of the child
(d) the special educational needs of the child
(e) the special education and related support services to be provided to the child to enable the child to benefit from education and to participate in the life of the school
(f) where appropriate, the special education and related services to be provided to the child to enable the child to effectively make the transition from pre-school education to primary school education
(g) where appropriate, the special education and related support services to be provided to the child to enable the child to effectively make the transition from primary school education to post-primary school education
(h) the goals which the child is to achieve over a period not exceeding 12 months.

The principal of the school has overall responsibility for implementing the individual education plan. Under the Act funds and supports are to be provided by the NCSE. Should a child transfer from one school to another, the principals of both schools should liaise with each other so that the plan is smoothly handed over.

Appeals

Designation of school is an issue dealt with under section 10 of the Act. The NCSE is responsible for ensuring that a child is designated to a suitable school in consultation with their parents/guardians. Boards of Management of a school can appeal a decision to send a particular child to their school if they feel they do not have adequate resources to cater for the needs of that child. Appeals are made to a special Appeals Board. The onus is on the school's board of management to prove lack of resources. Appeals must be dismissed or allowed within two months of being filed. If allowed, the NCSE must find a more suitable school for the child.

Each year a child's individual education plan must be reviewed by the principal (with inputs from relevant staff members and parents) and the findings of the review reported to parents and the SENO connected with the case. The purpose of the review is to evaluate whether the resources and services recommended in the plan have been put in place and whether or not the plan is working, i.e. are the goals of the plan being achieved? If, on receiving the report, the SENO believes that the plan is not working, he or she may call together the child's team or part of their team and amend the plan. Parents can request a review if they believe the goals of their child's plan are not being achieved. This can only be done if a review has not taken place in the previous six months and the request can be denied by the principal if they believe they have good reason. Parents can appeal this decision to the appeals board, where a decision will be made within one month.

Implications for Children with Special Needs

EPSEN is a major piece of legislation concerning children with special needs. In theory, children's needs are assessed on an individual basis and an appropriate plan put in place for them in a timely manner. In theory, children are allocated additional resources and services as needed. On the whole, it is widely believed that the Act has only been partially successful in meeting its own objectives. Many people in education feel that too much onus is placed on already overburdened principals (many of whom are in the classroom full-time) for this Act to be implemented properly. In addition, because of budgetary cut backs, supports and services are too scarce to implement individual education plans completely and thoroughly.

Equal Status Acts 2000 and 2004

The Equal Status Act 2000 promotes equality of opportunity for all citizens and legal residents of the state and prohibits discrimination on nine different grounds: gender, marital status, family status, sexual orientation, religion, age, disability, race or ethnic group. This piece of legislation has implications for many organisations including ECCE settings.

Implications for ECEC Settings

■   Settings must promote **gender equality**.

■   **Marital Status**

Settings must be mindful of marital status in their documentation, e.g. addressing correspondence to 'Ms' for all females. Practitioners should also be aware of the fact that that parents may have different surnames.

■   **Family Status**

Settings need to recognise that children may be part of a variety of family structures, e.g. nuclear, lone-parent or blended families. Settings should be inclusive of all these possibilities and ensure that their documentation and their education programmes positively reflect this reality.

■   **Sexual orientation**

Settings should be aware that some children may be living in households headed by same-sex couples. Settings should ensure that their recruitment policies and practices, documentation and education programmes positively reflect this reality.

■   **Religion**

Settings must be inclusive of all religions represented in the setting. Practitioners should consult with parents with regards to festivals of religious importance and they should celebrate them.

■   **Age**

Settings should promote a positive image of ageing. They should value the contribution that older members of society make, perhaps inviting grandparents into the setting to speak to children about life in the past.

■   **Disability**

Settings should be accessible to staff, children or parents with disabilities. In addition, positive images of persons with disabilities should be fostered in settings.

■   **Race**

There should be no discrimination on the grounds of race for entry to settings – for staff or children. In addition, diversity should be investigated and celebrated in settings.

■   **Ethnic background**

The Equality Act specifically mentions Irish Travellers in this section. There should be no discrimination on the grounds of ethnicity for entry to settings – for staff or children. In addition, ethnicity should be investigated and celebrated in settings.

Safety, Health and Welfare at Work Act 2005

This is the main piece of legislation dealing with all aspects of health and safety in the workplace. It sets out the rights and responsibilities of both employers and employees regarding health and safety in the workplace. The Act also allows for substantial fines to be imposed for breaches of the Act. On foot of the Act, the Safety, Health and Welfare at Work (General Application) Regulations 2007 came into effect on 1 November 2007. These provide details regarding health and safety requirements across a wide range of workplaces and they are very extensive. A short guide to the Act is provided by the Health and Safety Authority (HSA) and is downloadable online (www.hsa.ie). A summary of the areas of the Act relevant to childcare settings is given here.

Employer responsibilities include the following.

■   Manage and conduct all work activities so as to ensure the safety, health and welfare of people at work, including the prevention of improper conduct or behaviour likely to put employees at risk (e.g. bullying behaviour).

■   Design, provide and maintain a safe place of work that has safe access and emergency exits and uses equipment that is safe and without risk to health (e.g. suitable nappy changing tables).

■   Prevent risks from the use of any harmful article or substance (e.g. provide gloves for nappy changing).

■   Provide training so that employees can carry out duties safely.

■   Ensure there are correct accident reporting procedures in place.

Employee responsibilities include the following.

■   Take reasonable care to protect the health and safety of yourself and others in the workplace.

■   Do not engage in improper behaviour that will endanger yourself or others.

■   Never be under the influence of drink or drugs in the workplace.

■   Undergo any reasonable medical or other assessment, if requested to do so by the employer.

■   Report any defects in the place of work or equipment that might be a danger to health and safety.

Risk Assessment and Safety Statement

Under the Act, all employers are required to undertake a risk assessment and produce a safety statement for a workplace. The risk assessment should identify any potential risks to health and safety and the measures that should be put in place to deal with any such risks. A safety statement should be produced, which should be reviewed regularly. The short guide on the HSA website (see p. 58) provides a step-by-step guide to carrying out a risk assessment and creating a safety statement.

Protective Equipment and Measures

The employer should tell employees about any risks that require the wearing of protective equipment (e.g. using gloves for nappy changing).

Reporting Accidents

All accidents that occur in the workplace should be recorded in a specific book for the purpose. In a childcare setting, this is also important for child protection reasons. An employer is obliged to inform the HSA if an employee is off for more than three consecutive days as a result of a workplace accident.

Health and Safety Leave

An employer should carry out separate risk assessments in relation to pregnant employees. If there are particular risks to an employee's pregnancy, these should be either removed or the employee moved away from them (e.g. not asked to do any heavy lifting). Under Section 18 of the Maternity Protection Act 1994, if neither of these options is possible, the employee should be given health and safety leave from work, which may continue up the beginning of maternity leave.

Violence in the Workplace

The possibility of violence towards employees should be addressed in the safety statement, e.g. if there is a child in the setting with special behavioural needs. Proper safeguards should be put in place to eliminate the risk of violence as far as possible and the employee should be provided with appropriate means of minimising the remaining risk. The risk of robbery because of handling cash on the premises is another issue. Some settings ask parents to pay fees by standing order to eliminate this risk. Cash should be banked as soon as possible to reduce any risk of robbery.

Bullying, Harassment and Victimisation

It is an employer's duty to prevent improper conduct or behaviour (which includes bullying) in the workplace. An employer should have a set of procedures for dealing with complaints of bullying in the workplace and they should deal with such complaints immediately. Ignoring complaints of bullying could leave an employer open to a possible claim for damages by an employee. Employers also have an obligation to ensure that no employee is subjected to harassment on any of the nine equality grounds. In terms of victimisation, an employee cannot be penalised by their employer because they made a complaint under the Health and Safety Act (e.g. regarding bullying or harassment).

Department of Health and Children: Food and Nutrition Guidelines for Pre-School Services (2004)

This booklet was published by the Health Promotion Unit in order to promote healthy eating for pre-school children. It is available for download online. The Child Care (Pre-School) Regulations 2006 state that:

> A person carrying out a pre-school service shall ensure that suitable, sufficient, nutritious and varied food is available for a pre-school child attending the service on a full-time basis. (DoHC 2004:15)

This booklet aims to provide practical guidance in this regard and it is divided into six sections:
- Introduction
- Section 1: Children less than one year old
- Section 2: Children from 1–5 years old
- Section 3: Important issues
- Section 4: Healthy eating policy
- Section 5: Further information.

Introduction

The introductory part of this document provides a summary of key recommendations for pre-school services. These can be easily and quickly read and they are given in full opposite. This section also outlines how many meals and snacks children require in the day (depending on how long they spend in the service). The remainder of the document details how the key recommendations below may be realised.

Key recommendations include the following.

- Start with healthy eating for infants.
- Offer a wide variety of foods.
- Offer suitably sized portions.
- Offer healthy food choices and tooth-friendly drinks frequently.
- Accommodate special food needs of individual children.
- Plan healthy, varied meals and snacks.
- Help children to learn how to eat.
- Foster good dental health.
- Prepare food in a clean and safe way.
- Develop a healthy eating policy.

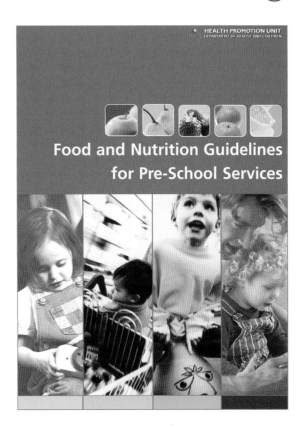

HEALTH PROMOTION UNIT
DEPARTMENT OF HEALTH AND CHILDREN

Food and Nutrition Guidelines for Pre-School Services

Section 1: Children Less Than One Year Old

Settings should accommodate mothers wishing to continue feeding breast milk to their babies. Breast milk should be stored in a refrigerator or freezer. It can be used to mix with food after weaning. Sometimes babies who are breast fed feed from a cup rather than a bottle, since feeding from a bottle requires a different suck and can cause difficulty feeding. If children are formula fed, parents should be encouraged to bring in feeds ready prepared. Feeds should be stored in the refrigerator (5°C) until ready for use. If formula feeds are made up in the setting, there should be an area specifically for that purpose. Feeds should be made up in exact accordance with the instructions on the formula container.

Infant feeding

- Babies should be held and have warm physical contact from an attentive adult while being fed. If possible, the same person should feed the baby each time.
- Babies should never be left with propped bottles, as this is dangerous and does not meet babies' emotional needs.
- Feeding bottles and expressed breast milk containers should be marked with the child's name and date.

- Keep milk feeds covered and in the fridge at 5°C. Store milk in the inside of the fridge (not in door shelves, which get warmer).
- Do not microwave the milk; warm it by standing it in a jug of hot water or in a bottle warmer. Do not leave milk in the warmer for longer than necessary.
- Defrost frozen breast milk by standing it in a jug of hot water for about 15 minutes. Shake it as it is thawing. Only defrost as much as is needed for that feed.
- If milk is heated in a jug of water, ensure the jug is in a safe place where children cannot get scalded by the water if it spills.
- Discard unfinished breast or formula milk after one hour. Let the parent know if the baby is leaving a lot of milk at feeds, so that he/she can bring the milk in smaller quantities.
- Bottles and teats should be thoroughly washed after use and sterilised, until the baby is 12 months old.

Weaning

Nowadays most babies have started weaning before they come into the ECEC setting. These guidelines recommended that bottle-fed babies are weaned aged 4–6 months and breast-fed babies are weaned aged 6 months. The guidelines offer other useful pieces of information about weaning.

- First foods should be puréed, soft–runny consistency, without lumps and introduced one at a time, leaving a few days between the addition of each new food (in case of allergies).
- Spoon the food into the baby's mouth gently and slowly so that the baby can suck the food from the spoon.
- Foods containing iron (including meat and iron-fortified cereals) should be started once the child is 6 months old, since the baby's birth reserves will be used by this age.
- Cereals (gluten-free for children under 6 months), fruits or vegetables are also suitable first foods. Use expressed breast milk, infant formula or cooled boiled water to mix foods.
- Clear instructions should be displayed for staff regarding any babies with allergies.
- Be patient: a baby is learning how to spoon feed and needs time to perfect skills. Do not rush feeding time.
- Breast milk or infant formula remain the central part of the diet until the baby is eating solid foods well or is about 12 months old.

The guidelines provide a very useful table showing suitable weaning (complementary) foods, their consistency, suitable drinks and foods to avoid for babies aged 4–12 months.

The guidelines also provide a very useful checklist for infant feeding.

Checklist for infant feeding		
Practice	Yes	No
1 Breastfeeding is encouraged: • Mothers are given a place to breastfeed • Parents are encouraged to bring in expressed milk		
2 Parents are encouraged to prepare their baby's feeds		
3 Expressed breast or formula milk is labelled with baby's name and date		
4 Expressed breast or formula milk is stored in the refrigerator at 5˚C or below		
5 Unfinished breast or formula milk is discarded after one hour		
6 Bottles are heated in a warmer or safely in a jug of hot water		
7 All feeding equipment is sterilised for babies under 12 months		
8 Infants are held by an attentive adult while feeding		
9 Food is spooned out of the jar, can or saucepan into a dish before feeding		
10 Unused food is stored according to manufacturer's instructions		
11 All preparation of feeds is done in a clean and safe manner		

Section 2: Children from 1–5 Years Old

The guidelines give an adapted version of the food pyramid (servings from each shelf vary with age) and recommend that this be used as a visual guide when planning children's meals.

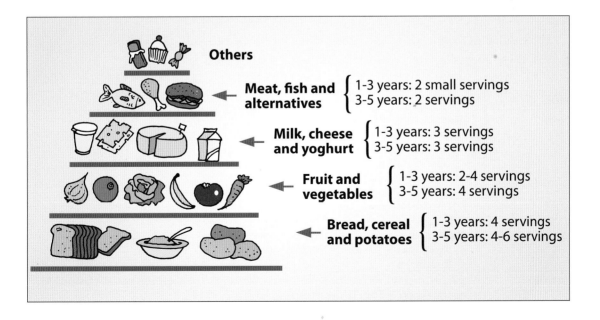

The food pyramid provides a good visual guide and emphasises the need for variety in the diet. The table below gives examples of servings from each shelf of the pyramid.

Recommended serving sizes	
Food group	**Serving sizes**
Meat, fish and alternatives	• 1 average-sized pork or lamb chop or homemade beef burger • 2 slices (60g) lean roast/boiled/grilled/ovenbaked meat or chicken/turkey • Medium-sized fillet of fish • 2 fish fingers • 2 eggs • 9 dessertspoons baked beans, peas or lentils
Milk, cheese and yoghurt	• 1 glass of milk (1/3 pint) • 1 carton of yoghurt • 30g hard cheese • 2 cheese slices • 1 bowl of milk pudding (100g) *Note: low-fat products should not be given to children aged 0–6*
Fruit and vegetables	• 1 medium-sized fruit (50g) e.g. apple, orange or banana • ½ glass pure unsweetened fruit juice, diluted well with water • 3 dessertspoons stewed or tinned fruit in own juices or fresh fruit salad • 3 dessertspoons chopped raw, salad or cooked vegetables • Small bowl of homemade vegetable soup
Bread, cereals and potatoes	• 1 slice of bread (white or wholegrain) • 1 small bread roll • 1 small bowl of breakfast cereal • 1 small scone (plain, wholemeal or fruit) • 1 medium potato (60g), boiled or baked • 3 dessertspoons boiled rice or pasta (80g)

The guidelines then go on to give suggestions for breakfast foods, main meals, snacks and drinks. These suggestions are very useful for settings while meal planning.

Meal	Suggestions

Breakfast	• Wholemeal or white bread
	• Scones or toast with butter or margarine
	• Porridge or breakfast cereals with milk
	   • Choose iron-fortified cereals
	   • Choose cereals without sugar, honey or chocolate coating
	   • Cereals with nut pieces are not suitable for young children because of the risk of choking and allergies
	   • Read the list of ingredients carefully
	• Fruit
	• Diluted unsweetened pure fruit juice
	   • Dilute one measure pure juice to 4/5 measures water
	   • Do not give tea

Main meals	• Boiled potatoes, pasta, rice, bread or other foods from the bottom shelf of the Food Pyramid provide the foundation for the meal. Include a food from this shelf at every meal, every day. • Wholemeal breads can be used for sandwiches – one slice wholemeal and one slice white bread makes a colourful sandwich for children. • A variety of fresh or frozen vegetables will add colour and texture to the meal as well as providing important vitamins and minerals. Offer a vegetable or fruit at the main meal every day. • Fresh fruit should be offered frequently. Use whole portions, half portions or fruit slices depending on the child's ability to handle the fruit pieces and their appetite.

Meal	Suggestions
Main meals *continued*	• Offer a milky food such as yoghurt, custard, cheese or a drink of milk. • A dish or recipe containing peas, beans, lentils, soya products or quorn makes a protein-rich meal for vegetarian children. Other children will enjoy it too. • Eggs can be used for meals also: scrambled, boiled, omelette or quiche. Ensure they are well cooked. • Use lean meat in cooking. However, if there is any visible fat, remove this before cooking. • Fish is good for children. Oily fish such as sardines and mackerel are also a good source of vitamin D for building healthy bones. Make sure all bones are removed from the fish. • Do not add salt in cooking and at the table.
Snacks	• Snacks help to meet the energy needs of the child. Do not fill children up with sugary snacks and drinks as this will dull their appetite for more nutritious foods. Nuts and popcorn are not suitable for children aged 0–5, due to choking risk. • Juicy snacks: oranges, pineapple chunks, plum (with stone removed), pear, tomato slices or cherry tomatoes, seedless grapes. • Smooth snacks: banana, yoghurt, milk puddings, homemade milkshakes and smoothies. • Crunchy snacks: raw vegetable sticks with yoghurt dips, apples, toast, breakfast cereals, crackers (not salty). • Chewy snacks: bread (rolls, pitta, baguettes, baps, scones), cheese slices, cubes or strings, cold meat slices.
Drinks (from 12 months upwards)	• Children should be encouraged to drink six or more cups of fluid per day. • If children do not drink enough fluid they will become constipated. • Children should feed from a cup from 12 months, since feeding from a bottle after this could encourage them to fill up on milk instead of eating more nutrient-dense foods; it may also lead to 'nursing bottle syndrome' or bottle rot. • Suitable drinks include whole cow's milk; goat's or sheep's milk (less allergenic than cow's milk); clean tap water; pure unsweetened fruit juice (diluted 1 juice to 4/5 parts water). • Flavoured milks should only be given occasionally, since they are usually sweetened. Fruit drinks and squashes (even sugar-free) are not suitable for young children. No fizzy drinks, tea or coffee.

Special Diets

If children have special food requirements it is up to their parents or guardians to inform the setting of this. Settings should have a section on the application form asking about special diet requirements. Sometimes children with complex food requirements (e.g. coeliac disease, PKU or diabetes) bring in their own foods and the setting reduces the child's fee accordingly. If food is to be prepared in the setting for children with special diets, then the setting needs to get all the relevant information from parents to ensure the child's needs are met. Relevant information will include information from the child's dietician.

Nut Allergies

Nut allergies can be quite severe. Children can have very serious reactions to even the tiniest piece of nut or even nut dust. They will usually wear an alert bracelet if this is the case. Most settings do not allow nuts or nut-based products into the settings at all. Even with this measure, settings have to be very vigilant to check all labels for nut or nut oils and to prepare the child's food in a separate area. Children with asthma, hay fever or eczema may find that nuts and nut products (e.g. peanut butter) make their condition worse. Children aged 0–5 should not be given whole nuts because of the choking hazard.

Vegetarian diets

Some children follow a vegetarian diet and their needs will have to be accommodated in the setting. There a number of such diets but the most common are:

- Lactovegetarians, who do not eat meat or fish but do eat animal products such as milk, cheese and eggs
- Vegans or strict vegetarians, who eat only plant foods such as fruit, vegetables, nuts, cereals and soya milk.

As a rule, parents or guardians of vegetarian children (especially vegans) will also be vegetarians themselves and so will be a good source of information regarding suitable foods.

- Lacto-vegetarians should include plenty of nutrient-rich foods in their diet (e.g. cheese, milk, yoghurt and eggs), since these are a valuable source of protein, calcium and vitamin A.
- Meat alternatives such as Quorn, textured vegetable protein (TVP), tofu and pulse vegetables (peas, beans and lentils) should be included in main meals as a good source of protein.
- Red meat is one of the best sources of iron in a non-vegetarian diet. Vegetarians can get their iron from other sources such as green vegetables, eggs, dried fruits and fortified breakfast cereals.
- Vitamin C should be plentiful in the diet in order to help with the absorption of available iron.

Food Customs of Different Cultures and Religions

In the interests of equality and diversity, it is important to acknowledge the eating customs of different cultures and religions. Food customs may specify what foods are eaten, how the foods are prepared, what combinations of foods are used or when particular foods are eaten. In addition to this, settings should consult with parents about celebration foods that could be introduced in the setting as part of multicultural education. The table above is given in the nutritional guidelines for pre-schools and may be useful, although in reality some of the foods may be difficult to source (particularly in rural areas).

Kosher Foods

Kosher foods are foods that follow the Jewish dietary laws (from the Bible). Pork, rabbit, eagle, owl, catfish, sturgeon and any shellfish, insect or reptile are non-kosher. Other species of meat and fowl must be slaughtered in a prescribed manner to be kosher. Meat and dairy products may not be made or consumed together. A kosher food that is processed or cooked together with a non-kosher food, or any derivative of a non-kosher food, becomes non-kosher. For example, food colouring derived from a shellfish and used in a cake makes the cake non-kosher.

Food customs					
Food	**Jew**	**Sikh**	**Muslim**	**Hindu**	**Buddhist**
Eggs	No blood spots	Yes	Yes	Some	Some
Milk/yoghurt	Not with meat	Yes	Not with rennet	Not with rennet	Yes
Cheese	Not with meat	Some	Some	Some	Yes
Chicken	Kosher	Some	Halal	Some	No
Mutton/lamb	Kosher	Some	Halal	Some	No
Beef	Kosher	No	Halal	No	No
Pork	No	Rarely	No	Rarely	No
Fish	With scales, fins and backbone – no shell fish	Some	Halal	Some	No
Nuts, pulses, fruit, vegetables	Yes	Yes	Yes	Yes	Yes

Halal Foods

Halal foods are foods that are permitted under Islamic law. Halal meat is obtained by slaughtering the animal in a particular way (by slitting its throat with a very sharp knife so that the animal dies quickly) and then hanging the animal so the blood drains from it. Non-halal foods can only be eaten under Islamic law if there is no other food available.

Children's Food Requirements

Children's food requirements will depend on the length of time they spend in the setting daily. The nutrition guidelines for pre-school children make the following recommendations.

Children in Full Day Care (more than 5 hours)

Offer at least two meals and two snacks, e.g. breakfast, snack, lunch and snack. One meal should be a hot meal. If children are there for a long day, an evening meal may also need to be provided. Make sure parents are aware of what children have eaten so that they can offer children more food if necessary at home. Do not assume that the child has had breakfast; ask parents and give breakfast if this is the arrangement.

Children in Day Care for up to 5 hours (maximum) Per Session

Offer at least two meals and one snack, e.g. breakfast, snack and lunch. It is not necessary to have a hot meal. However, the meal should be balanced, including items from every shelf on the food pyramid.

Children in Day Care up to 3.5 hours Per Session (including Afterschool Care)

Offer one meal and one snack, e.g. snack and lunch. Children who attend the pre-school for other short periods generally do not have a meal. However, choose nutritious snacks for this group.

Cooking and Presenting Food

Food should be cooked using healthier methods of cooking such as casseroling, roasting, boiling, stewing, steaming, baking, stir frying and grilling instead of shallow or deep frying. If oils are used, choose polyunsaturated (e.g. Flora oil). Present foods in small, attractive portions. Try to make sure dishes are as colourful as possible (e.g. serving shepherd's pie with garden peas and carrots). Ensure that dishes include a variety of textures (e.g. smooth and crunchy). Finger foods can be provided for children learning to self-feed. Salt should be absolutely avoided. Fresh stock is best but if stock cubes must be used, choose low-salt variety. Season dishes with herbs rather than salt. Cost-effective, highly nutritious meals can be produced by buying vegetables in season and using cheaper cuts of meat (just as nutritious), provided correct cooking methods are used.

A sample weekly menu is given in Appendix 3 (see p. 189) as is a blank template (see p. 190). The guidelines provide a list of suitable well-balanced main meals which include:

- Homemade beef burgers (grilled or oven baked), oven chips and vegetable or salad
- Pork pieces in a casserole served with pineapple and rice
- Beef casserole with carrots and potatoes
- Savoury mince with peas and mashed potatoes/pasta shapes
- Roast chicken with carrots/parsnips and roast potatoes
- Grilled fish pieces (without batter) with sweet corn and rice
- Mince, lentils or chickpeas with stir-fried vegetables and rice
- Chicken pieces in a casserole served with broccoli and potatoes
- Lasagne made with minced beef, chicken, lamb, fish or beans/lentils and vegetables
- Lamb casserole with carrots/turnips and potatoes
- Mince, lentil or bean shepherd's pie with vegetable or salad
- Tuna chunks with sweet corn and carrots in a cheese sauce served with pasta
- Fish in white sauce served with rice and green beans
- Salad with chunks of cooked fish or chicken, grated carrot, lettuce, chopped tomato and cooked pasta
- Winter vegetable casserole with carrots, turnips and potatoes, topped with grated cheese and breadcrumbs
- Fish chunks, cauliflower and baked potato in a tomato sauce, served in the baked potato shell
- Chicken risotto served with green vegetables
- Mince made into a meatloaf served with mashed potatoes/pasta shapes and carrots
- Stir-fried vegetables (mainly pulses) with rice/egg noodles
- Macaroni and cheese served with sliced tomato or a green vegetable
- Wholemeal cheese and egg quiche with cooked green vegetables or salad
- Vegetable burger with carrots and mashed potatoes

■ Cauliflower cheese with peas and boiled potatoes

■ Thick homemade soup (e.g. lentil, vegetable or chicken) served with a bread roll and cheese, followed with some whole or sliced fruit.

(DoHC 2004: 28)

The guidelines also provide a checklist for managers to assist them in providing nutritious, attractive meals for children in the setting.

Checklist for menu planning		
Practice	Yes	No
1 Are 2–3 healthy meals and 2–3 healthy snacks offered daily?		
2 Do main meals include food from each shelf of the food pyramid?		
3 Does food look pleasing on the plate: small attractively presented portions, variety of colour and texture?		
4 Are parents given an opportunity to make suggestions for menus?		
5 Are menus for the week displayed or copies given to parents?		
6 Are children with special dietary requirements catered for?		
7 Are religious or cultural requests observed?		
8 Is there a designated person responsible for promotion of nutrition in the setting?		
9 Are food safety guidelines followed at each stage of food preparation process?		
(Adapted from DoHC 2004: 29.)		

Section 3: Important Issues

There are three important issues dealt with in this section of the guidelines.

■ Helping children learn to eat (including fussy eaters)

■ Fostering good dental health

■ Safe preparation and storage of food (see p. 113)

Helping Children Learn to Eat

The pre-school years are a very important time and children should be encouraged to develop good eating and exercise habits. When children are learning to self-feed they do make a mess. Settings need to allow for this and give plenty of time, also encouraging children to sample as many foods as possible. Child-sized utensils, crockery, tables and chairs may also make it easier for children to self-feed. Children need to be closely supervised while eating. A feeding cup is recommended for children over 12 months, rather than a bottle. Older children should be encouraged to help with meal preparation and table setting.

Use mealtimes as an opportunity to talk about food, where it comes from and how it benefits our bodies. Encourage good table manners. Practitioners need to be good role models both in terms of their own table manners and by eating a variety of healthy foods. Give children sufficient time to eat and never force children to eat. Most children at some time or other go through periods of food refusal. This is normal and unless it is very prolonged it is nothing to worry about. In order to encourage children to eat healthily, the guidelines make a number of recommendations including:

- Serve meals at regular times so children know when to expect food.
- Sit with children while eating: mealtimes should be social events and children learn from adults.
- Do not give children 'empty calories' foods that may interfere with appetite.
- Keep portions small and attractive: children can always ask for more but may be turned off by large amounts on their plates.
- Children's appetites are not constant: if children are having an off-day or week, it is usually no cause for alarm.
- Sit 'fussy eaters' with children who are good eaters.
- Allow children to self-feed and offer them finger foods.
- Do not force children to eat – if they do not wish to clear their plate, this is fine.
- Do not bribe children (e.g. if you eat your dinner, you can have ice cream). This is giving the wrong message.

Fostering Good Dental Health

The fostering of good dental health is of utmost importance in the early years. If children's 'baby teeth' decay, this can have implications for their permanent teeth: if baby teeth have to be removed, this can cause spacing problems with adult teeth. Also, habits built up in early childhood tend to continue into later childhood and beyond.

Prolonged use of a bottle can result in 'bottle rot' or nursing bottle syndrome. This is when the lactose in the milk changes into sugar (because of the digestive enzymes in the mouth). The lactose provides a food source for bacteria in the mouth, which in turn produces acid and rots the teeth. Introduce a cup or beaker for children aged 6 months and aim to stop bottle feeding from 12 months.

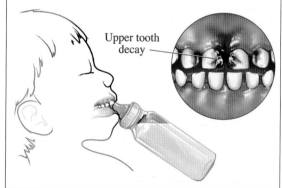

Tooth decay is linked with the frequency and the amount of sugar in the diet. Sugary foods and drinks should not be provided. Practitioners should be alert to hidden sugars: look out for the words sucrose, glucose, maltose, fructose and dextrose on food labels (these are all sugar). Tooth erosion (wearing of tooth enamel) can also be caused by a high consumption of acidic foods: do not serve undiluted fruit juice or fizzy drinks.

Children should be given foods such as raw apples, carrots, crusts, toast and other foods in a form that encourages chewing. This increases the flow of saliva and cleans the teeth. Children should be encouraged to brush teeth after meals using a very soft brush and a mild paste. Sometimes practitioners see parents engaging in practices that are not good for their child's dental health. Practitioners should be sensitive in relation to this matter. However, it is important to inform parents of the following facts.

- Pure fruit juices, sweetened tea, diluted drinks (e.g. MiWadi) should not be given to children in a bottle, as this causes tooth decay.
- Soothers or bottle teats should not be dipped in honey, sugar, etc.
- Rusks or baby rice should not be put in babies' bottles.
- Babies should not be put to bed with a bottle, as this causes nursing bottle syndrome and is a choking hazard.
- Sugary foods or drinks, if they are to be given, should only be given with or after meals. Do not provide them on their own: they dull appetite and stick to teeth, providing a food source for teeth-rotting bacteria.

Section 4: Healthy Eating Policy

Because people can have different interpretations of what healthy eating means, it is important to have a healthy eating policy agreed between practitioners and parents. If settings consult with and involve parents, they are much more likely to have support and compliance with the policy. Childcare settings are responsible for *all* of the food eaten on their premises, so it is important that parents are clear on what children may or may not bring with them. Parents should be given a written copy of the policy. A sample policy is given as part of the guidelines and is included in Appendix 4 of this book (see p. 191).

Food for Special Occasions

Settings, particularly if they are big, could have a celebration every other day of the week. It is therefore not feasible or indeed recommended that sweet foods (e.g. birthday cakes) be served as part of celebrations. Children can be made feel special in other ways.

- They can choose the story of the day.
- They can be given a crown to wear.
- They can be given a sticker on their jumper (birthday boy or girl).
- They can be given a round of applause.
- They can have their birthday acknowledged on the 'birthday calendar'.

Outside Catering Companies

Many settings, due to lack of facilities or personnel, employ outside catering companies to supply their main meals. If this is the case, catering companies should be able to meet guidelines and provide varied, nutritious meals suitable for children of different ages. They should provide a menu cycle in advance and food should be prepared and delivered in accordance with food safety guidelines.

Learning Through Food

Meal times should be a learning experience for children. For example, while children are drinking a glass of milk they should be told: 'Milk helps your bones grow big and strong.' Food is also a good way of introducing children to different cultures and traditions.

Food can be used as part of the early years curriculum. The guidelines provide very useful suggestions as to how this may be done.

- Participate in national healthy eating campaigns.
- Use foods (e.g. dried pasta and pulses, rice and seeds) in creative activities.
- Cut out food pictures from magazines for collages.
- Have tasting sessions of various fruits and vegetables.
- Make food prints using halved small potatoes, carrots, apples or parsnips.
- Make a seed ball for the birds.
- Have a pretend play café or shop.
- Grow mustard seeds, cress or sprout seeds.
- Make papier-mâché fruit and vegetables.
- Encourage the children to draw pictures of healthy foods, e.g. Kieran Kiwi, Olivia Orange or Bart Broccoli playing in the garden.
- Organise a display of raw fruit and vegetables and ask children to identify them using fun names.
- Sing food-related songs and rhymes, e.g. 'Ten juicy apples hanging on a tree...'
- Play food-smelling games, using foods such as vinegar, oranges or onions.
- Play food-tasting games where the children have to guess what foods they taste without seeing what they are eating.
- Let children help to prepare food, depending on age and ability. Remember to encourage boys and girls to be involved.
- Ask the children to think of the many ways in which we use milk, cheese and yoghurt each day. Explain that these foods are rich in calcium, which is good for bone health.
- Ask the children to name all the foods they associate with the word 'snack'. You can talk through with the children which choices are healthy and which are not so healthy. This game can be used to highlight the topic of dental health with young children.

(DoHC 2004: 40)

Physical Activity

The last part of this section concerns physical activity. Active children have a better appetite.

Playing outside in summer sunshine helps children to get vitamin D for healthy bones and teeth, although it is important to limit exposure in strong sunlight and to use hats and sunscreen as necessary. Physical activity builds up muscle strength and fitness and develops skills of balance, co-ordination and climbing. Active children are more likely to be active adults; active lifestyles reduce the risk of ill health. Physical activity should be timetabled into every day. In fact, many influential educationalists (e.g. Froebel, Steiner and Montessori) advocated that children should be free to choose when they engage in physical activity throughout the day. These educationalists advocated that children should have free access to a garden area and should not be confined to specific times for outdoor play. Practitioners in forest schools, where children spend much of their day in a woodland environment, highlight the advantages of the outdoor environment for increasing children's appetites and physical activity.

Section 5: Further Information

This section provides names, addresses and phone numbers of useful contacts regarding food and nutrition for pre-school services. These include:
- Community nutrition and dietetic services
- Pre-school health inspection teams.

Full details can be accessed at http://www.dohc.ie/publications/pdf/HPU_pre-school_guidelines.pdf?direct=1.

Infectious Diseases Regulations (1981–2011)

While this piece of legislation is primarily aimed at health professionals such as GPs, it also has implications for organisations working with children (such pre-schools and crèches). The regulations list a number of infectious diseases. If these diseases are suspected, the HSE must be informed; medical practitioners will do this. If a child or worker in a crèche or pre-school contracts one of these infectious diseases, there may be certain protocols that will have to be followed to ensure the health and safety of staff and children attending the service. Protocols followed will depend on the nature of the infectious disease and will be explained by HSE staff. Appendix 5 (see p. 193) lists the notifiable diseases and their causative pathogens.

Protocol for Infectious Disease

An example of a protocol for meningitis is given here. In the rare event that there is a case in your setting, you must be prepared to manage the situation as effectively as possible. If you suspect that a child in your care is displaying any of the signs and symptoms of meningitis, the following protocol must be followed.

1   Act immediately to get urgent medical attention by contacting the child's GP, taking the child straight to the nearest Accident and Emergency department or dialling 999.

2   Contact the child's parents and inform them of your concerns and your actions. Inform them that you need to escort the child to hospital if the parents are some distance away.

3   HSE personnel who specialise in the public health management of infectious diseases will give you official notification if public health action is required. You will be advised of further appropriate action to take as each case is treated individually.

4   Usually there is no reason to close the early years setting. However, some parents may choose to keep their children at home.

5   There is no need to destroy or disinfect any equipment or toys that the child has touched.

6   The HSE will liaise with the person in charge of the early years setting to offer advice and guidance at all times.

7   The HSE will usually issue a letter to other parents to let them know about the situation and to give information on meningitis.

8   In cases of meningococcal disease, antibiotics may be offered to persons considered to be close contacts. These are usually immediate family members or household contacts. Antibiotics are given to kill the bacteria that may be carried in the back of the throat; this reduces the risk of passing the bacteria on to others. In certain situations, a vaccine may be offered. These actions are co-ordinated by the HSE.

9   The likelihood of a second case of meningitis is extremely small. However, if two or more cases occur within four weeks in the same early years setting, then antibiotics will usually be offered to all children and staff by the HSE. During this time you should remain alert to the signs and symptoms. Parents should be advised to contact their GP if they are concerned that their child is unwell.

10   If a child is taken ill at home and meningitis is suspected, you may be contacted by a parent or carer to let you know of the illness and the HSE may also contact you.

(Source: The Meningitis Trust.)

'Infection and Schools – a Manual for School Personnel' is a booklet produced by the HSE. It has useful information on any aspects of infectious disease, including the following.

- Infection: what it is, who gets it, how it is transmitted and how do we fight it?
- Infection control policies: identifying the chain of infection, immunisation, excluding the infection source, interrupting transmission, hand washing, food handling, education and communication, first aid, blood precautions, management of vomit.
- Specific infectious diseases: gastrointestinal, respiratory, direct contact, blood, vaccine preventable diseases.

The appendices of this booklet include useful contacts and websites, sample letters to parents, guidelines for visitors to open farms, hand washing guidelines, hand washing poster, etc. The booklet can be downloaded at www.healthpromotion.ie/hp-files/docs/HPM00406.pdf.

Data Protection Acts 1988 and 2003/Freedom of Information Acts 1997 and 2003

These Acts and their amendments concern personal data held on computer or manual file by organisations, including schools and pre-schools. In general, personal information must be:

- Obtained and processed fairly
- Kept for a specific purpose (e.g. applying for extra resources for a child with SEN)
- Used only for that specific purpose
- Kept secure and safe
- Kept accurate and up to date
- Adequate, relevant and not excessive
- Retained no longer than necessary.

Under the Acts, organisations must give a copy of their personal data to an individual on request.

Síolta

Síolta is the name given to the National Quality Framework for Early Childhood Education in Ireland. Síolta was published in 2006, having been developed by the Centre for Early Childhood Development and Education (CECDE) on behalf of the Department of Education and Skills (DES). Basically, Síolta provides a guide or roadmap for all types of ECEC settings in order to help them provide a quality early education service for the children in their care.

Unlike some countries, Ireland's ECEC sector has (for the most part) developed in a very organic way. The education and care of pre-school children has not traditionally been seen as the responsibility of the Irish state. For this reason, the ECEC sector in Ireland is very diverse. Young children (0–6 years) are educated and cared for in a wide range of settings, including day care services, childminding services, sessional services and infant classes in primary schools. Services may be run by the DES, private companies or individuals, or community or voluntary groups. Practices within these services may be informed by varying theoretical perspectives: Montessori, Steiner, Froebel, etc.

The purpose or rationale behind Síolta is to recognise this diversity but also to provide a general quality framework so that all providers know how to:

- Define a quality service
- Evaluate the service they are currently providing
- Plan for improvement of their particular service.

Since the publication of Síolta in 2006, many ECEC settings and individual practitioners have engaged informally with the framework, using it to reflect on their practice and to plan for their own improvement of services. Settings also have the option of formally engaging with Síolta by undertaking the full Síolta Quality Assurance Programme (QAP), supported by a Síolta co-ordinator. The Síolta QAP is designed to provide guidance and support for ECEC services that wish to seek external assessment of their service against the Síolta standards and components of quality.

Structure of Síolta

Síolta is composed of three elements:
- 12 principles
- 16 standards
- 75 components.

The 12 *principles* give us the 'overall picture' of the main elements of quality ECEC. The 16 *standards* and the 75 *components* provide detail on what the practitioners actually need to do in order to put the framework into practice.

Síolta has four user manuals. There is one user manual for each of the following:
- Full- and part-time day care
- Infant classes
- Childminding
- Sessional services.

All of these manuals can be found at http://www.siolta.ie/access_manuals.php.

Síolta Principles

There are 12 Síolta principles, which are described below.

- **The value of early childhood**

  Early childhood is a significant and distinct time in life. It must be nurtured, respected, valued and supported in its own right.

- **Children first**

  Children's individuality, strengths, rights and needs are central in the provision of quality early childhood experiences.

- **Parents**

  Parents are the primary educators of children and they have a pre-eminent role in promoting children's wellbeing, learning and development.

- **Relationships**

  Responsive, sensitive and reciprocal relationships, which are consistent over time, are essential to the wellbeing, learning and development of young children.

- **Equality**

  Equality is an essential characteristic of quality ECEC.

- **Diversity**

  Quality ECEC settings acknowledge and respect diversity and ensure that all children and families have their individual, personal, cultural and linguistic identity validated.

- **Environment**

  The physical environment of young children has a direct impact on their wellbeing, learning and development.

- **Welfare**

  The safety, welfare and wellbeing of all children must be protected and promoted in all ECEC environments.

- **The role of the adult**

  The role of the adult in providing quality early childhood experiences is fundamental.

- **Teamwork**

  The provision of quality early childhood experiences requires co-operation, communication and mutual respect.

- **Pedagogy**

  Pedagogy in early childhood is expressed by curricula (or programmes of activities) that take a holistic approach to the development and learning of children and reflect the inseparable nature of care and education.

- **Play**

  Play is central to the wellbeing, development and learning of the young child.

Síolta Standards and Components

Síolta has 16 *standards* or areas of importance in a quality setting. Each of these standards is broken down into a number of more specific *components*.

Each component includes sections entitled *signposts for reflection* and *think about*. These sections give practitioners ideas as to how they can meet the requirements of the component. This is where the user manuals can differ from each other. There will be some differences between the suggestions made for different settings, e.g. infant classes and childminding services.

Standard 1	Rights of the child
Standard 2	Environments
Standard 3	Parents and families
Standard 4	Consultation
Standard 5	Interactions
Standard 6	Play
Standard 7	Curriculum
Standard 8	Planning and evaluation
Standard 9	Health and welfare
Standard 10	Organisation
Standard 11	Professional practice
Standard 12	Communication
Standard 13	Transitions
Standard 14	Identity and belonging
Standard 15	Legislation and regulation
Standard 16	Community involvement

Example of Standard and Component

Standard 15: Legislation and Regulation

Being compliant requires that all relevant regulations and legislative requirements are met or exceeded.

Component 15.1

All relevant legislation and regulations are met or exceeded by the setting.

Signposts for Reflection/Think About

15.1.1

Is your service compliant with relevant legislation and regulations?

Think about:
■ Employment
■ Equality
■ Health and safety
■ Building and planning
■ Data protection.

15.1.2

Do you have a named person who understands and accepts responsibility for ensuring the service complies with relevant legislation and regulations?

15.1.3

What procedures do you have in place to ensure that the setting keeps up to date with new legislation and regulations?

Using Síolta

It would be impossible for an ECEC setting to tackle all of the areas identified by Síolta at once. This is why Síolta recommends that settings stand back, look at all of the 16 standards and then decide which standard they will tackle first, second, etc.

Once the setting has decided which standard they wish to tackle first, they should:
■ Go to the relevant section of the colour-coded manual to find the chosen *standard* and the components that accompany it.
■ Select the *component* they wish to tackle first.
■ Go to the relevant page to find the chosen component and the sections that go with it: *signposts for reflection* and *think about*.
■ Read the *component, signposts for reflection* and *think about* sections carefully.
■ Think about what is currently being done well in the setting in relation to this component. Acknowledge what is being done well: write it down.
■ Record ideas about what should be done to improve practices related to this component.
■ Create a written action plan based on these areas for improvement.

Below is an example of a small section of an action plan. The standard being examined is Standard 12: Communication. The component is 12.1.

Example of an Action Plan

Standard 12: Communication
Component 12.1

Component	What we are doing well	Areas for improvement	Timeframe	Person responsible
Component 12.1 The setting undertakes the collection of relevant and appropriate information on all children and stores it in a safe manner	Application form obtains information on: • Contact details • Collection arrangements • Health • Food preferences and allergies	Need to keep information up to date: review the information bi-annually	Bi-annually	Child's key worker
	Information is stored alphabetically in a locked filing cabinet	N/A	N/A	N/A
	Cabinet can be unlocked quickly in case of an emergency	N/A	N/A	N/A
	Child observations are carried out	Child observations need to be carried out in a regular, systematic way	At least one observation per child per week (more if required)	Child's key worker (supervisor, if key worker needs a second opinion)
	Most observations are completed to a professional standard	Observations to be reviewed together by staff and crèche manager before filing, with constructive feedback given	Ongoing	Crèche manager with co-operation of all staff
		Closer relationship between observation and programme planning	Ongoing	Child's key worker
		Parents invited to view observations at pre-arranged times	Ongoing	Crèche manager

Síolta produces a newsletter approximately once a year. Issues of the newsletter can be found at www.siolta.ie. (Look under the 'What's New' section.)

Aistear

Aistear is the National Curriculum Framework for children aged 0–6 years in Ireland. Aistear was developed by the National Council for Curriculum and Assessment (NCCA) in partnership with the early childhood sector in Ireland and abroad. Aistear was published in 2008.

Aistear states its own purpose, which is to:

...provide information for adults to help them plan for and provide enjoyable and challenging learning experiences, so that all children can grow and develop as *competent and confident learners* within loving relationships with others. Aistear describes the types of learning (dispositions, values and attitudes, skills, knowledge, and understanding) that are important for children in their early years, and offers ideas and suggestions as to how this learning might be nurtured. The framework also provides guidelines on supporting children's learning through partnerships with parents, interactions, play, and assessment. (NCCA 2009: 6)

Structure of Aistear

Aistear is presented in four documents or booklets. All four documents can be found at www.ncca.biz/Aistear. In addition to this, NCCA have produced a series of audiovisual presentations on all aspects of Aistear. The presentations can be viewed and listened to on the same website. (Look under the 'Aistear Toolkit' section.)

The four Aistear documents are:

- **User Guide**
  This is a 24-page document that gives a broad outline of the purpose of Aistear, information on how it works alongside other developments in the sector (e.g. Síolta) and planning for the implementation of Aistear.

- **Key Messages from the Research Papers**
  This eight-page document gives a very general summary of the key pieces of research that informed the development of Aistear. A link exists within this document to the research papers in their full form.

- **Guidelines for Good Practice**
  This 118-page document details how an environment can be created to facilitate children's learning and development. It describes how to create an environment that allows the principles and themes to be realised.

■   **Principles and Themes**

This 59-page document details what should be included in an early childhood curriculum framework.

Principles and Themes of Aistear

This document details what should be included in an early childhood curriculum framework. Aistear identifies 12 *principles* of early learning and development. These principles are presented in three groups.

Group 1: Children and Their Lives in Early Childhood

■   The child's uniqueness
■   Equality and diversity
■   Children as citizens

Group 2: Children's Connections with Others

■   Relationships
■   Parents, family and community
■   The adult's role

Group 3: How Children Learn and Develop

■   Holistic learning and development
■   Active learning
■   Play and hands-on experiences
■   Relevant and meaningful experiences
■   Communication and language
■   The learning environment

Each principle is presented using a short statement. This is followed by an explanation of the principle from the child's perspective. This explanation highlights the adult's role in supporting children's early learning and development.

Below is an example of one of the principles presented in Aistear.

Example of a Principle
The Child's Uniqueness (Principle 1)

Each child has his/her own set of experiences and a unique life-story. He/she is an active learner growing up as a member of a family and community with particular traditions and ways of life.

■ Remember that I am a unique individual with my own strengths, interests, abilities, needs and experiences. Recognise and build on these when you are helping me to learn and develop.

■ You know I am a confident and able learner and that I learn at my own rate about things that interest me. Support me to do this in a way that allows me to make decisions about what I learn and when, and how well I am learning.

■ I need you, my parents and practitioners, to share what you know about me with each other. By doing this, you can get to know me better and plan things for me to do that will help me to learn in an enjoyable and meaningful way.

■ In order for you to understand and support me you need to understand my family background and community. This is especially important if I come from a disadvantaged or marginalised community.

(NCCA 2009: 7)

The 12 Aistear principles describe the characteristics of a quality early learning environment. Aistear then goes on to describe *what* children should learn: dispositions, attitudes and values, skills, knowledge and understanding.

Aistear's curriculum framework is organised under four *themes*:
■ Wellbeing
■ Identity and Belonging
■ Communicating
■ Exploring and Thinking.

Each theme begins with a short description of its importance for children as young learners. The theme is then organised into four *aims*, with each aim further divided into six *learning goals* (with some goals being more suitable for older children).

Aistear also provides some suggested ideas for the types of learning experiences that adults might provide for children while working towards learning goals. These ideas are known as *sample learning opportunities*. They are presented for three overlapping age groups:

- Babies (0–18 months)
- Toddlers (12 months–3 years)
- Young children (2½–6 years).

See Appendix 6 (p.196) for an example of an Aistear theme (Identity and Belonging), along with its aims, learning goals and the sample learning opportunities available for one age group – babies.

Guidelines for Good Practice

The Guidelines for Good Practice document is divided into four main sections. Each section describes a different aspect of pedagogy. Pedagogy means the holistic development and education of children and young people.

The Guidelines for Good Practice are made up of:

- Section 1: Building partnerships between parents and practitioners
- Section 2: Learning and developing through interactions
- Section 3: Learning and developing through play
- Section 4: Supporting learning and development through assessment.

The guidelines then go on to demonstrate what good practice might look like in the four areas above. This is done through the use of a number of *learning experiences* or practical, everyday examples.

Section 1: Building Partnerships between Parents and Practitioners

Partnership Benefits Everybody

This section of the Good Practice Guidelines outlines what partnership means and describes how parents and practitioners can work together to enhance children's learning and development. When good partnerships exist, everybody benefits.

How Are Good Partnerships Created and Maintained?

Aistear's Good Practice Guidelines provide very practical guidance and suggestions as to how good partnerships can be created and maintained between practitioners and parents. The guidelines take the unusual but very effective step of providing examples of *learning experiences* in order to illustrate partnership in action. Aistear's Good Practice Guidelines focus on four ways for parents and practitioners to work together.

- Supporting learning and development
- Sharing information (e.g. settings can produce a monthly newsletter)
- Contributing (e.g. parents can volunteer to assist when the setting goes on an outing)
- Making decisions and advocating different approaches and courses of action (Aistear recognises that parents know their own children better than anyone else, so it makes sense to involve parents in any decisions about their children).

Section 2: Learning and Developing Through Interactions

Aistear recognises that relationships are at the very centre of early learning and development. Section 2 of the Good Practice Guidelines identifies a range of interaction strategies and methods that adults can use to enhance children's learning and development. Effective interactions between adults and children need to be *'respectful, playful, enjoyable, enabling, and rewarding'* (NCCA 2009: 27).

Interaction Strategies

The guidelines offer detailed information on the following four strategies:
- Building relationships
- Facilitating
- Organising
- Directing.

Of the four interaction strategies, the first two (building relationships and facilitating) are very much child led, while the last two (organising and directing) are more adult led.

Building Relationships

With this strategy children learn by being with others, exploring with them, and taking on risks and challenges with them. As part of this strategy, it is the responsibility of the adults to create an environment to allow this interaction to happen. The child directs and co-directs their own learning.

Facilitating

As part of this strategy, children learn through activities that they have initiated for themselves. The child is encouraged to take or share the lead with adults.

Organising

Children learn effectively when they are in a well-planned, well-resourced environment. The role of the adult is to plan and maintain this environment while systematically reflecting on their practice and ensuring that the environment is of the highest quality.

■   **Directing**

Children learn through planned and guided activities that build on their interests and experiences. This strategy allows children to 'develop particular dispositions, values and attitudes, skills, knowledge, and understandings' (NCCA 2009: 28).

Aistear examines the four interaction strategies and then goes on to provide *sample methods* for each strategy. These sample methods are a very useful resource – see pp.31–51 of the guidelines.

Section 3: Learning and Developing Through Play

Aistear recognises the value of play in early learning and development. Section 3 of the Good Practice Guidelines deals with the subject of play and its role in the early childhood curriculum. Play is examined under various headings:

■   What is play?

■   Are there different types of play?

■   Where do children play?

■   What is my role as the adult in play?

■   How do I prepare the play environment?

■   How do I help children who find it difficult to play?

■   How can I use play across Aistear's four themes?

What is Play?

Aistear describes play as 'ways of doing' and then goes on to further define it by describing ten of its characteristics.

■   **Active**

Children use their bodies and minds in their play. They interact with the environment, with materials and with other people.

■   **Adventurous and risky**

Because of the pretend element of play, children are more comfortable taking risks and being more adventurous.

■   **Communicative**

Children share information and knowledge through their play. This can be done verbally or non-verbally.

■   **Enjoyable**

Play is fun, exciting and humorous.

■ **Involved**
Play is deeply absorbing. Children become completely focused on their play, concentrating and thinking about what they are doing.

■ **Meaningful**
Children play about what they have seen and heard, and what they know. Play helps them to build upon and extend their knowledge, understanding and skills in a way that is enjoyable and natural to them.

■ **Sociable and interactive**
Children can play alongside or with others. Sometimes they need to play alone.

■ **Symbolic**
Children imagine and pretend while playing. They try out skills, ideas, feelings and roles. They re-enact the past and rehearse the future, e.g. pretending to 'read' and 'write' before they can actually do so.

■ **Therapeutic**
Play can be very beneficial for children to express and work through emotions and experiences. This is the basis of the work of a play therapist.

■ **Voluntary**
Children choose to play. Their play is spontaneous.

Types of Play

There are many different types of play and children are often involved in more than one type at any one time. For example, children could pretend they are cooking dinner (pretend play) while using play-dough to create vegetables, meat and potatoes (manipulative play). It is important that children experience a good variety of play types in order to support their learning and development across the four Aistear themes: Wellbeing, Identity and Belonging, Communicating, and Exploring and Thinking.

Aistear outlines five broad categories of play and gives a brief description of each:

■ Creative
■ Games with rules
■ Language play
■ Physical play (including exploratory, manipulative and constructive)
■ Pretend play (including dramatic, make-believe, fantasy, early literacy and numeracy, small world and socio-dramatic).

Play can also be defined by *who* is involved in the play.

■ *Solitary play* means that the child plays alone. This is a dominant feature of younger children's play, especially children aged 0–2.

■ *Spectator* or *onlooker play* is also a feature of younger children, although older children who are very shy or in an unfamiliar setting may also engage in this type of play. Here, the child watches others at play but does not engage directly in it. Children can get great enjoyment out of this type of play and they should not be pushed into joining in. This play is typical for children aged 2–2½.

■ *Parallel play* (also called *adjacent play* or *co-action*) involves the child playing separately from others but close to them, sometimes mimicking their action. This type of play is seen as a transitory stage: from solitary and onlooker types of play to a more socially mature associative and co-operative type of play. This play is typical for children aged 2½–3.

■ *Associative* or *partnership play* happens when children begin to play together, developing interactions through doing the same activities or playing with similar equipment, or through imitating. This play is typical for children aged 3–4.

■ *Co-operative play* happens when children interact, take turns, share and make decisions about how and what to play. They collaborate, develop and negotiate ideas for their play. This type of play requires advanced levels of social maturity and organisational skills and is therefore more common in children aged 4–6 onwards.

Where Do Children Play?

Children will play anywhere, but it is important that children have good access to well-equipped indoor and outdoor play areas. It is important (within reason) that children can go outside if and when they wish to do so. It is ideal if indoor and outdoor play areas adjoin each other.

Given the unpredictability of Irish weather, some preparation is required for this to be possible. Children should have wellies, waterproof jackets and a change of clothes available in the setting. This will ensure that they can play outside in all types of weather. Aistear suggests that settings should actually embrace Irish weather and learn to work with it. This could mean having a rainy-day box 'that includes umbrellas, sieves, toy boats, toy ducks, containers for measuring rainfall, funnels, charts for recording the level of rainfall, containers for gathering water to recycle (to water flowers and plants indoors, for example), tin foil (for making hats), tapes to measure the size of puddles, and relevant picture books' (NCCA 2009: 55).

The Role of the Adult in Children's Play

Aistear states that, in order for adults to play an important role in children's play, they must fully appreciate and understand the importance of play and its usefulness as a learning tool across all areas of the early years curriculum. Aistear examines the role of adults under three headings.

■ *Planning and Preparing the Play Environment*

This means giving children a wide variety of rich play possibilities.

■ *Supporting Play*

Aistear emphasises that the role of the adult in children's play is very much a facilitative rather than a directive one.

■ *Reviewing Play*

Through various methods of observation and assessment (see below), the adult gathers a wide variety of information about children's play. This information should be used for planning and extending children's future play experiences and for making decisions about the play environment.

How Can the Adult Help Children Who Find it Difficult to Play?

Aistear recognises that, while all children can play, some may require extra support from the adult to benefit fully from play. Children who are impulsive or children who get into conflicts easily may find it difficult to play. Children who are withdrawn or isolated may also face challenges. There are likely to be children whose first language is different from the language of the setting. There may be children who have speech delays and children who have sensory or physical impairments. These children often need more specialised and focused support from the adult.

The role of the adult is to carefully observe what is going on and to plan accordingly. Depending on the nature of the difficulty, the adult can use many different strategies. The adult can change the physical or social environment. They can introduce a buddy system among the children. They can break down activities into smaller, more doable, parts. They can provide one-on-one support for some children and they can use special equipment or devices to help children with particular special needs.

How Can the Adult Use Play Across Aistear's Four Themes?

The adult can plan the play environment so that children use different types of play to support their learning and development. Play can be used to incorporate Aistear's four themes: Wellbeing, Identity and Belonging, Communicating, and Exploring and Thinking.

The Good Practice Guidelines demonstrate how play can be used across Aistear's four themes. The guidelines present a total of 16 *learning experiences* to show how this can be done. Four learning experiences are presented for each Aistear theme: one for babies, one for toddlers, and two for young children. See pp. 60–9 of the Good Practice Guidelines for these 16 learning experiences.

Below is an example of one learning experience that shows how play can be used to develop the themes of Aistear.

Example of a Learning Experience

Learning and Developing Through Play
Theme: Wellbeing
Aim 2
Learning Goal 3
Age group – Toddlers: sessional service (special pre-school) and full- and part-time day care (nursery)

The toddlers in the nursery spend a lot of time outdoors all year round. Some of the children who are quite shy and timid inside become much more active and enthusiastic outside. They run, climb the ladder, go down the slide, kick a football, play in the outdoor café, get fuel for their vehicles at the pumps, play with the water and sand, and cycle their tricycles. The staff members play *hide and seek* with them, organise races, play football, join them for a latte in the café, and chat about what they are doing and learning. On cold days they all dress up warmly in their coats and hats before going outside, and on wet days they splash in the puddles in their wellies and listen to the rain fall on their tinfoil covered umbrellas.

Daniel (almost 3 years) attends a special pre-school three mornings a week. He joins the children in the toddler room in the nursery on the other two days. He can't move any of his limbs so is reliant on the staff to carry him outside. He squeals with delight when they lift him up in the air and when they put him on the slide. The staff talk to Daniel, building up and reinforcing his language, spatial awareness and physical skills, saying, for example: 'Now Daniel, you are up, up, up...now down, down, down.' They place Daniel on the ground and put a ball beside his head. He gets great pleasure from moving the ball slowly with his head and getting it right under the bench. They say: 'Well done, Daniel ...under, under the bench.' These physical experiences help Daniel's gross-motor development and enable him to understand spatial concepts like over/under, up/down and in/out. The other children regularly run over to Daniel and gently push the ball to him or wave at him. He smiles and giggles when they do this.

Reflection
Do all children in my setting have opportunities to get involved in and enjoy play?

(NCCA 2009: 60)

Section 4: Supporting Learning and Development through Assessment

The final section of the Aistear Guidelines for Good Practice describes what assessment is and shows how assessment can be carried out in early childhood settings.

Aistear defines assessment as:

> …the ongoing process of *collecting, documenting, reflecting on*, and *using* information to develop rich portraits of children as learners in order to support and enhance their future learning.
> (NCCA 2009: 72)

Broadly speaking, there are two types of assessment:
- Assessment **of** learning
- Assessment **for** learning.

It is important for practitioners to fully understand the difference between these two types of assessment and also to appreciate the purposes and uses of both.

Assessment of Learning

This is the type of assessment that has been traditionally used by our education system. Children are given various tests and assessments and the results are collected and reported. In pre-school settings, observations are carried out and findings are compared to norms for the child's age group. In primary schools, standardised tests are given. In Ireland, these include the Drumcondra Primary Reading Test (DPRT) and the MICRA-T (Mary Immaculate Reading Attainment Test). In secondary schools, end of year tests are used alongside major exams, such as the Junior Certificate and Leaving Certificate.

All of these tests are examples of assessment *of* learning. The purpose of this is to gather data about a child's progress and to use this data to inform others about the child's achievements. However, nowadays this form of assessment alone is seen as insufficient. It should not be the only form of assessment carried out with children in any setting or age group. Assessment of learning can also be called *summative assessment*, i.e. a summary or report of the child's progress to date is provided.

Assessment for Learning

Generally, with assessment *for* learning, assessment is part of the learning *process*. It is not something that happens at the end of learning, i.e. testing what has been learned. Assessment for learning can also be called *formative assessment*, i.e. the intention is to form, shape or guide the next step in learning.

Assessment for learning (AFL) is always forward-looking. With AFL, the practitioner always shares the *learning intention* (learning goal) with the learner. The teacher then helps the child to unpack the learning intention, assisting them to understand exactly what it is they are being challenged to learn. As the child progresses through the learning experience, the adult gives the child feedback that is quite focused. This feedback gives the child a clear picture of what they are doing well and it also helps them plan for how they can further progress their learning.

What is Assessed?

Assessment enables the teacher to gain a lot of valuable information about children and their learning. They gain information about:

■ **Children's Dispositions**

Children's dispositions or personality characteristics have an impact on their learning. Children's dispositions will affect their concentration, perseverance, curiosity, willingness to try new things, positivity, resilience and tolerance.

■ **Children's Skills**

Children's ability to learn will be affected by their skills in many different areas. These include the following skills.

■ Physical skills, e.g. walking, climbing, cutting and writing
■ Intellectual skills, e.g. memory, problem-solving and concept formation
■ Language skills, e.g. listening, understanding, speaking, reading and writing
■ Emotional skills, e.g. emotional regulation, emotional security, self-esteem and self-concept
■ Social skills, e.g. interacting effectively with others, moral development and understanding social norms.

■ **Children's Knowledge and Understanding**

Children's knowledge and understanding of the key aspects of the curriculum (e.g. Aistear or the primary school curriculum) will affect their learning.

■ **Developmental Milestones**

Children's development is uneven, e.g. a single child may have very advanced language skills but undeveloped physical skills. Children's development does not happen at the same rate for each child, either. Despite this, developmental milestones do exist and they are useful. These developmental milestones can help ECEC practitioners to notice early signs of potential difficulties. Practitioners can bring their concerns to parents and help them to contact other educational and health professionals.

Purpose of Assessment

Assessment is carried out for many reasons. In the ECEC setting, assessment can be carried out in order to:

- Understand where individual children are in terms of their physical, intellectual (cognitive), language, social and emotional development, so that activities are both developmentally appropriate and challenging for them
- Evaluate how well children are achieving the aims and goals of the early years curriculum
- Record children's learning, so that parents can reinforce and support this learning at home
- Inform parents about their children's developmental progress, which may help with the detection of early signs of developmental delay
- Observe children exhibiting problem behaviours, so that frequency, triggers and the response of staff can be investigated
- Allow children to reflect on their own learning and to discuss what motivates them and what they are interested in learning in the future
- Allow the teacher to reflect on their own teaching and to have the opportunity to try new activities, change routines, re-arrange the setting or use new resources
- Keep vital information on children aged 0–3 (and beyond this if the child has special needs), since parents may need exact information (e.g. on fluid intake) if the child becomes ill and needs medical attention.

How Can Assessments Be Documented?

Samples of Children's Work

Children should be encouraged to create a portfolio of their work. Portfolios can take the form of a scrapbook or folder in which pieces of work are kept. Photographs of larger pieces (e.g. construction pieces) can be taken and these can also be kept in the portfolio. Children should be involved in choosing which pieces go into their portfolio. Sometimes children like to bring home certain artworks and display them there. They should be allowed to do so, since a photograph or photocopy can be kept in their portfolio.

ICT

Once parental permission is given, photographs, video and audio recordings can be used to document children's learning and development. Practitioners can use video recordings in particular to observe groups of children while they are involved in activities. Sometimes, during the hustle and bustle of an activity, it can be difficult for practitioners to observe and evaluate learning. ICT helps practitioners with this reflective practice.

Daily Diaries or Records of Care

Practitioners (usually key workers) can make notes in a communications copy or other diary. The diary can be used to record lots of information regarding an individual child's care routines, e.g. what and how much they ate, when they slept and when they were changed. Notes regarding the child's daily activities can also be included in the diary, together with photographs of the child on particular days. The diary can be sent home to parents in the evening.

Checklists

The practitioner can use pre-prepared checklists in order to record particular aspects of children's learning and development. If the templates for checklists are planned carefully, the checklists can be very useful tools for recording all kinds of development, e.g. pre-writing skills.

Observation Notes and Records

Practitioners observe the children in their setting all the time. Observations can be recorded quickly (in the form of brief notes) or in more detail. Various observation methods can be used and they will have corresponding reports. Time samples, event samples, narrative observations and pre-coded language observations can all be very useful.

How Can Assessments Be Stored?

Central Files

It is vital that central files containing certain types of information about children be kept in a secure location in the setting. It is advisable to have an office in the setting and a fireproof filing cabinet that can be locked. The information in the central files can include such things as: parents' names and contact details, medical information and copies of reports from other professionals, e.g. physiotherapists. Usually, there is a separate file for each child and the files are alphabetically arranged in the cabinet. While it is important that this information is securely kept, it is also important that staff members have access to the information when required. In addition to hard copy (information printed on paper), settings may have information stored on computers. Computers should be password protected.

Learning Portfolios

Each child in the setting should have an individual learning portfolio into which selected samples of their work are stored. Portfolios can take the form of a folder, scrapbook or box. Again, children should be involved in decisions about what goes into their learning portfolio. This will encourage them to think about the quality of the work they are producing and the amount of effort they are putting into it. Photographs of larger pieces (e.g. construction pieces) can be taken and these can also be included.

Practitioner Files

In most settings, children have one key worker. Key workers should have a practitioner file for every child assigned to them. This may take the form of one big lever arch file with coloured dividers separating each child's information. Key workers can record all sorts of valuable information: observation notes, attendance records and records of conversations with parents or other staff members. The information in practitioner files may be transferred to the central file at the end of the year.

Methods of Assessment

Traditionally, assessment was seen as something that was very much adult led. More recently, however, early years practitioners are beginning to value more child-led assessment methods. Nowadays, child-led assessment is used alongside traditional assessment methods.

Five assessment methods will be examined in this section:

- Self-assessment (child led)
- Conversations (child led)
- Observation (adult led)
- Task setting (adult led)
- Testing (adult led).

Self-assessment

Self-assessment is a very important aspect of learning. When self-assessment goes well, children are able to think about what they have done, said or made. They can then reflect on what they would like to do differently or better next time.

In order for self-assessment to be worthwhile, children must have a clear idea of what it is they are trying to achieve. In this way, they have a yardstick with which to measure their work. Assessment can be measured in terms of learning goals.

Adults can set learning goals for children and these learning goals can be defined by What I'm Looking For (WILF). For example, the adult says: 'We are going to cut out the circle, square and triangle shapes as carefully and as neatly as we can.'

Sometimes, children can set their own goals. Adults have an important role in helping children clarify their own learning goals by providing resources to give the children ideas and by asking prompting questions.

Once children are clear on their learning goals, they will be able to start working through them and their learning will benefit greatly. Adults can help children to self-assess again. They can do this by asking questions that prompt the child to self-evaluate.

Conversation

Conversations between adult and child are very much a part of all assessment methods (with the exception of testing, where very little conversation takes place). Conversations are a useful part of assessment when the adult can employ various conversation strategies. These strategies give the adult a better of understanding of what children can do and understand. Some strategies are listed below.

■ Open Questions

These questions should be used most often, since they invite the child to think and elaborate on their answers. Examples of open questions include:
■ Have you any ideas?
■ Why do you think that happened?
■ How did you do that?
■ What were you thinking when…?

■ Closed Questions

These questions are limited in terms of the response they require from children. These questions ask the child for short, factual answers. Closed questions should not be used all the time but they can be useful to get the conversation going. Examples of closed questions include:
■ What colours did you use?
■ Did you enjoy building the bricks?
■ Which is your favourite picture?

■ Thinking Out Loud

Sometimes, if the adult 'thinks out loud' about a problem, this can prompt children to offer their opinions and suggestions. In this way, the adult can assess the children's understanding of particular concepts. For example, a teacher is transferring water from one vessel to another using a small spoon. The teacher says: 'This is going to take ages! I will have to think of a better way to do this.' This encourages the children to offer suggestions.

■ Expressing an Opinion

Children should be encouraged to offer an opinion and to justify it. For example, a teacher is reading a story during circle time. The teacher says: 'I think Paul was very selfish in this story. What do you think, Lara?'

■   **Listening to Children's Conversations**

Practitioners should listen carefully to children's conversations while the children are at work together. Valuable information can be learned about children's knowledge and understanding. Notes on these conversations should be recorded.

Observation

Observation involves carefully watching and listening to children while they are involved in their daily activities and routines. Information gathered through observation is very important, since it gives practitioners information about (1) what children know and can do already and (2) what children *almost* know and can almost do. In other words, observation informs practitioners about the next steps for a child's learning.

There are a number of different observation methods that may be used, depending on what it is the practitioner wishes to find out. Observations may be planned or spontaneous. It is always better if observations are carried out by someone who knows the child very well, e.g. a key worker.

There are many different methods of observation:
■   Narrative or storytelling
■   Pre-coded
■   Checklist
■   Time sample
■   Event sample
■   Movement or flow charts
■   Tables, pie charts and bar charts
■   Photographs, audio and video recordings.

When practitioners are studying for their qualifications in college, they are asked to carry out a number of observations as part of certain modules (e.g. child development). These observations are often very detailed and take a huge amount of time to complete. This level of observation is not possible in the workplace: the practitioner would have little time to do anything else!

In the workplace, the emphasis is on *usefulness*. The aim of the practitioner is to record *accurate*, *useful* information about a child or group of children and their learning. The practitioner then uses this information to inform their work with the children. In this way, observation is a critical part of the learning process.

Task Setting

Since children learn by doing, task setting is a useful way of assessing children's learning. Additionally, task setting is one of the principal tools of *assessment for learning*. Adults sometimes set tasks after a period of time or they may set a piece of work or a project for children after they have done work on a particular topic.

In order for task setting to be successful, children need to know exactly what it is they are being asked to do. They need to be 'let in on the marking scheme', so to speak, so that they have a clear idea of what is required for success.

For example, Tony has set up an obstacle course outside for the children to use. He believes that the course will be useful for encouraging gross-motor skills and also social skills (e.g. waiting patiently for one's turn). Tony takes a group of six pre-school children out on the course. He demonstrates how to complete each part of the course (the children copy what he does). The children then take turns completing the course on their own. Tony shows them how to time each other with a stop watch. Throughout the process, the children learn by doing.

Testing

In the early years curriculum, observation is the most common form of assessment used. Testing is not commonly used in the pre-school setting, but it may be used by health or other educational professionals in the pre-school when they are working with children suspected to have a special need. Commercially produced standardised tests are used by some professionals in order to test particular aspects of children's development, e.g. motor skills, social skills, language skills and behaviour. Results of tests are usually represented by comparing scores with those of other children the same age.

Health and Safety

This section covers the following areas related to health and safety:

- Safe resting and sleeping
- Child protection
- Illness
- Exclusions
- Immunisation
- Medications
- Nappy changing and toilet time
- Accidents
- First Aid
- Spillages
- Safe play environment

- Food hygiene
- Arrivals and departures
- Anti-bullying
- Fire/disaster plan
- Safety statement.

Safe Resting and Sleeping

The Child Care (Pre-School) Regulations 2006 and the National Standards for Pre-School Services 2010 (standard 14) give clear guidelines regarding safe resting and sleep. Additional requirements need to be met in the case of overnight services (see Appendix 7 on p. 200).

Example of Outcome and Criteria

Standard 14: Sleep

Outcome
Each individual child's need for sleep or rest is facilitated.

Criteria
14.1 A 'safe sleep' policy is in place, including policy in relation to overnight services where applicable.

14.2 The service facilitates each individual child's need for sleep or rest and liaises with parents in relation to children's sleep patterns/needs. Children are allowed to sleep or rest when they are tired and not just at designated times.

14.3 Children are provided with suitable sleeping facilities away from general play areas.

14.4 If the sleep area for babies is accommodated in the baby room, the overall space measurements of the baby room should be 4.2 square metres per child. (The accommodation of the babies' sleep area in the baby room should only be considered when the group size is six babies or fewer.) The sleep area should be away from other activities.

14.5 Where reasonably practicable, sleep rooms should have a viewing panel that allows resting or sleeping children to be within the sight of staff at all times.

14.6 Lighting via windows or light fixtures should be controlled to maintain a subdued lighting level conducive to sleep while also allowing sleeping children to be monitored.

14.7 Children under two years of age should have access to a standard cot. Children over two years of age should have access to sleep mats, stacking beds or suitable alternatives. Linen must not be shared – separate linen must be available for each child.

14.8 The temperature of sleep areas should be maintained at between 16°C and 20°C.

14.9 Cots, beds, etc. should be positioned so that they are not directly adjacent to a heat source, curtains, window blinds or anything else that might pose a risk to the child.

14.10 Sufficient space must be allotted to each cot/bed to allow staff unhindered access to each child, and also to reduce the risk of infection.

14.11 A sleep log must be maintained for babies and children under two years of age to record the checks made on sleeping children. The log should record times, the person who checked the baby, and his or her signature. Checks should be made every ten minutes.

14.12 A member of staff must be present in the sleep room at all times when the numbers of children sleeping warrant it, or where a particular safety risk is identified.

14.13 Sleep facilities must comply with fire safety requirements as set out by the relevant Local Authority.

(National Standards for Pre-School Services 2010: 22–5)

Safe Sleep

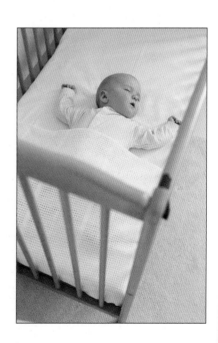

- Babies should be put to sleep on their back. Older babies and children may change position themselves during sleep, but should be put down on their backs.
- Feet to foot – babies' feet should be at the bottom of the cot.
- Use sheets and aerated blankets, not fluffy or bulky duvets. Tuck sheets and blankets securely, but not tightly. Use a firm, clean, well-fitting mattress.
- Make sure babies' heads remain uncovered during sleep.
- There should be no pillows, toys, cot bumpers or other items in the cot with a baby.

Child Protection

Every ECEC setting should have a written child protection policy. It should be informed by:

- Childcare Act 1991 (see p. 29)
- *Children First: National Guidance for the Protection and Welfare of Children (2011)* (see p. 35)
- *Our Duty to Care: The Principles of Good Practice for the Protection of Children and Young People (2002)* (see p. 49)
- National Standards for Pre-school Services (Standard 11).

Child Protection

Standard 11

Outcome

Children are safely cared for within the service. Any concerns coming to the attention of the service which relate to the safety and welfare of those children, either within or outside the service, are responded to in accordance with Children First: National Guidance for the Protection and Welfare of Children.

Criteria

11.1 All adults working in the service, and/or those who have access to children attending the service, have been appropriately vetted in accordance with Regulation 8 [of the Child Care (Pre-School) Regulations 2006].

Regulation 8 states that a person carrying on a pre-school service must ensure that all staff, volunteers and students are fully vetted before commencing work with children. Vetting involves:

- Garda or police vetting (for people who have lived outside this state)
- At least two references (one from a recent employer); these have to be checked and validated
- If the person has had no previous work experience (e.g. a student), a reference must be obtained for a reputable source (e.g. college course co-ordinator).

(Child Care (Pre-School) Regulations 2006: 42)

11.2 A written child protection policy is in place, and all adults working and looking after children in the service have received induction training on the policy and are familiar with it.

11.3 The written child protection policy reflects the requirements of *Children First: National Guidance for the Protection and Welfare of Children* and clearly outlines arrangements for contact with the local Health Services Executive Child Protection Team (including contact names and telephone numbers).

11.4 The policy and procedures clearly set out staff responsibilities for the reporting of suspected child abuse or neglect.

11.5 A designated senior member of staff, together with a deputy, has received 'Keeping Safe' training in child protection, and is responsible for liaising with the relevant agencies in any child protection situation.

All staff are aware of:
- The vigilance required to remain alert to child protection and welfare needs
- The symptoms of children at risk of abuse
- Their responsibility to report any concerns without delay
- Their responsibility to report to the designated senior member of staff (or deputy) any other staff member behaving inappropriately towards a child
- The requirement for confidentiality in all such cases.

(National Standards for Pre-School Services 2010: 19)

Illness

There are a number of different guidelines and factors that should be followed when a staff team is developing an illness policy. A number of the Child Care (Pre-School) Regulations 2006 are very relevant to illness, as is Standard 12 (Healthcare) of the National Standards for Pre-School Services 2010. Both of these documents need to be read thoroughly before compiling an illness policy.

Regulation 13 (register of pre-school children) indicates that as part of the registration process a detailed account of any medical issues a child has needs to be accurately given and recorded. In addition, this same regulation requires that up to date contact details must be given and maintained for parents of each child enrolled. This information is vital should a child become ill during hours of operation. A record of each child's immunisations must be given and recorded, along with consent for the administration of emergency medical treatment. Contact details for each child's GP must also be given and recorded.

Regulation 14 (records) reiterates this and also advises that if medication is to be administered in the setting, there must be a signed parental consent form indicating this. Some children may be on continuous medication (e.g. a child with cystic fibrosis may be on a low-dose antibiotic or a child with epilepsy may be on an anti-epileptic drug). If this is the case, settings need to have clear written instructions from the child's medical practitioner and also have a clear policy regarding who administers the medication and how its administration is recorded. In contrast to children with an ongoing medical need, most settings do not accept children into the setting when they are unwell (see exclusion policy below). If a child becomes unwell during the day, some settings may administer non-prescription medications such as anti-febrile agents (temperature lowering, e.g. Calpol) while at the same time contacting parents to have children collected as soon as possible. If this is the case, written permission to do this plus a record of administration should be maintained.

Illness Prevention

A number of the Child Care (Pre-School) Regulations 2006 are concerned with preventing the spread of infection and also providing a physical environment conducive to health.

- **Regulation 18: Premises and facilities**
  This regulation requires that there is adequate space per child, that the premises and equipment is kept hygienically clean and that it is protected from infestation. Special attention is paid to rodent-proofing the setting. Health and safety should not be compromised either by the rodents themselves or methods chosen to eliminate them (e.g. poison or traps). Separate laundry facilities are required for the hygienic laundering of bedding and towels.

- **Regulations 19 and 20: Heating and ventilation**
  Infection and illnesses are far less likely to spread in settings that are properly heated (not too hot) and ventilated.

- **Regulation 22: Sanitary accommodation**
  This regulation requires that there are adequate nappy changing and disposal facilities on the premises, adequate toilet and hand washing facilities with soap, thermostatically controlled hot water and a suitable and hygienic means of hand drying. Sanitary accommodation should not communicate directly with any occupied room or food room. This regulation is very important for illness prevention.

- **Regulation 25: Equipment and materials**
  This regulation requires that soiled items (e.g. bedding, clothes, towels) should be stored separately for laundering and that settings should have a cleaning schedule in place for all areas of the setting. A template for such a rota is given in the appendices of the guidelines.

- **Appendix G**
  Appendix G of the Child Care (Pre-School) Regulations 2006 gives details of a number of other preventative measures. Settings should have an adequate number of potties for the number of children being toilet trained (preferably one each) and there must be a programme for their rigorous cleaning and disinfection. Hand washing routines must be in place and adults must enforce them, especially after toileting. The highest standards of

hygiene must be adhered to by staff. If there are animals or pets on the premises, care must be taken to ensure that the health, safety and welfare of children is not put at risk (Standard 12). Outdoor sand boxes must be covered to prevent the risk of animals defecating in them.

When all of these factors are considered, staff should sit down and write out an illness policy for the setting. An illness policy like any other policy is really a written account of how a particular issue is dealt with by the setting. The first draft of the policy should be given to parents to read; they can provide feedback before the policy is finalised. When settings are inspected by HSE personnel, this offers another opportunity to perfect policies. Inspectors will have seen examples of good practice during the course of their work and they will be able to make suggestions for improvement.

Exclusions

There are certain situations whereby for health and safety reasons children need to be excluded from the setting. It is important that an exclusion policy is developed so that parents understand the reasons for exclusion and that all cases are treated in the same way. All children must be treated equally. An exclusion policy could include some of the following points.

- Children with infectious illnesses should not attend the service.
- In order to limit the spread of infection, if a child becomes ill during the night, they should not be brought to the service the following day.
- If a child is kept away from the service due to an infectious illness, the service should be informed in order to monitor other children who may have been exposed.
- In the case of certain infectious illnesses, the service will inform by letter parents whose children may have been exposed to such illnesses. Confidentiality will be respected.
- If a child becomes ill while attending the service, parents will be informed immediately and the child must be picked up without delay. The child may have to be removed sensitively from the group and, under supervision of a staff member, be kept in a separate area until collected.

Some services will add policies or information specific to particular infectious illnesses: meningitis (bacterial and viral), chickenpox, measles, head lice, mumps, ringworm, rubella, scabies, scarlet fever, strep throat, threadworms, whooping cough, etc. New conditions will need to be added as time goes on, e.g. swine flu, Norovirus (winter vomiting bug). While exclusion policies usually relate to infectious illness, exclusion also relates to children who are displaying extremely challenging behaviour.

Immunisation

Immunisation remains one of the most effective strategies to combat spread of infectious diseases. Immunisations break the chain of infection by eliminating the susceptible host (someone to carry and pass on the infection). This approach has been successfully implemented for previously common infections of childhood, e.g. polio, diphtheria, tetanus. Immunisation involves giving a killed germ, a live but weakened germ or just a critical part of the germ to a susceptible person. This then causes an activation of the person's immune system and results in their immunity to that specific germ. In April 2011, the HSE produced a new booklet: 'Your Child's Immunisation Booklet'. The booklet gives parents very clear information on all aspects of immunisation. In a pocket at the back of the booklet is a fridge magnet (detailing Ireland's schedule of immunisation) and an 'immunisation passport', in which details of children's immunisations can be recorded.

Schedule of immunisations in Ireland*		
Age	**Where**	**Vaccine**
Birth	Hospital /clinic	BCG
2 months	GP	6 in 1 + PCV
4 months	GP	6 in 1 + Men C
6 months	GP	6 in 1 + Men C + PCV
12 months	GP	MMR + PCV
13 months	GP	Men C + Hib
4–5 years	GP/school	4 in 1 + MMR
1st year of secondary School	School	HPV (Girls only)
6th year of secondary School	School	HPV (Girls only)
11–14 Years	School	Tdap

Key:
- BCG: Bacille Calmette-Guerin (Tuberculosis vaccine)
- 6 in 1: Diphtheria, haemophilus influenzae B (Hib), hepatitis B, pertussis (whooping cough), polio and tetanus
- PCV: Pneumococcal vaccine
- Men C: Meningococcal C
- MMR: Measles, mumps, rubella
- Hib: Haemophilus influenzae B
- 4 in 1: Diphtheria, tetanus, polio, pertussis (whooping cough)
- HPV: Human papillomavirus
- Tdap: Tetanus, low dose diphtheria, accelular pertussis

Correct at time of press.

As part of the enrolment process, settings should have an accurate record of the immunisations that children have received. Parents could be requested to produce the child's immunisation passport if available and the setting's information should be recorded from this. Settings usually do not exclude children who have not received any/all immunisations, but should be on the alert if there is a case of an infectious disease in the setting.

Medications

Policies regarding medication need to address a number of different issues. Again the Child Care (Pre-School) Regulations 2006 and the National Standards for Pre-School Services 2010 should guide policy development. The following factors should be considered when compiling a policy relating to medications.

- Information regarding each child's healthcare needs is sought from parents when the child is enrolled. This information is accurately recorded, securely but accessibly stored and updated as necessary.
- Written permission is obtained from parents regarding the administration of first aid and in relation to the seeking of any necessary emergency advice or treatment.
- A clear protocol for the administration of medication, both prescribed and non-prescribed, including the administration of an anti-febrile (temperature lowering) medication should be written and followed.
- Prescription medications are not administered to a child unless parents provide written instructions from a medical practitioner regarding their administration. Medications will not be administered unless they have been prescribed for that particular child.
- All medications are stored out of the reach of children.
- If the administration of prescribed medicines requires technical or specialist knowledge, individual training specific to the child concerned is provided for staff.

Sample Anti-febrile Agent (Temperature Lowering) Medication Consent Form

I give ☐

I do not give ☐

permission to Cheeky Monkeys crèche and pre-school to administer temperature lowering medication, i.e. Calpol (paracetamol) or Nurofen (ibuprofen), to _____ if he/she becomes unwell with a temperature of 38°C or over.

I understand that the service will contact me before administering the medication and I will pick _____ up without delay upon being contacted.

Signed: _____
(Parent/guardian's signature)

Please print name: _____

Anti-febrile Agent (Temperature Lowering) Medication Record Sheet						
Child's temperature	Date and time	Medication given	Dosage	Administered by	Witnessed by	Signature of parent/guardian

Nappy Changing and Toilet Time

Regulation 22 (sanitary accommodation) of the Child Care (Pre-School) Regulations 2006 recommend the following in relation to nappy changing and toileting.

- Adequate, suitable and hygienic nappy changing facilities must be in place.
- Separate toilets should be provided for adults where necessary (one toilet and one hand basin per eight adults).
- An adequate number of hand basins with running cold and thermostatically controlled hot water, soap and suitable means of drying at or near the sanitary accommodation and nappy changing area (one toilet and one hand basin per ten toilet-using children).
- The sanitary accommodation and nappy changing area should not communicate with any occupied room or food room, except by means of a hall, corridor, ventilated lobby or space.
- Adequate and suitable facilities for the safe and hygienic storage and disposal of soiled nappies must be in place.
- A shower/bath facility for washing, with thermostatically controlled hot water and a designated area for sluicing soiled garments should be provided in full day care services.

Regulation 24 (waste storage and disposal) stipulates that waste must be hygienically stored and disposed of frequently. It must not be accessible to children. There should be a strict cleaning programme in place for the thorough cleaning of toilet and nappy changing areas.

Nappy Changing

Taking all of these regulations on board, settings will need to come up with a specific care routine for nappy changing. All new members of staff need to be trained in relation to this routine to ensure continuity and quality of care. The routine will clearly explain:

■ How often nappies are to be checked
■ How often nappies are to be changed (if not soiled)
■ How nappies are to be changed with particular emphasis on safe, hygienic practices
■ Filling of nappy changing log.

Nappy changing log			
Time	Wet	Soiled	Products applied/observations
9.30	✓		Vaseline applied
10.20	✓	✓	Vaseline applied, stools very loose
1.00	✓		Vaseline applied
2.15	✓	✓	Vaseline applied, stools very loose
3.30	✓		Vaseline applied
5.30	✓		Vaseline applied

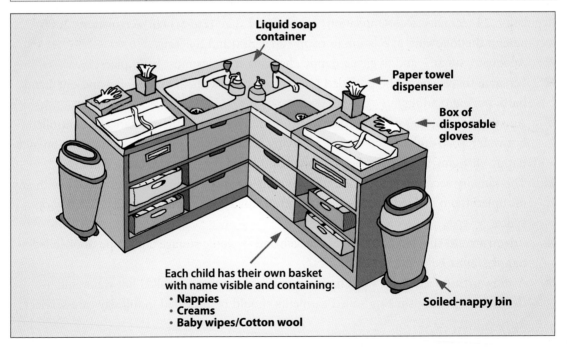

Liquid soap container

Paper towel dispenser

Box of disposable gloves

Soiled-nappy bin

Each child has their own basket with name visible and containing:
• Nappies
• Creams
• Baby wipes/Cotton wool

A nappy changing room should have the following facilities:

■ Safe, hygienic nappy changing table – with straps
■ Two sinks if possible – one for hand washing and one for sluicing soiled clothing (to be put in plastic bag for collection by parents)

- Shelving for changing materials
- Nappy bin
- Steps so that older children can climb safely onto nappy changing table.

Toileting Young Children

Depending on the nature of the setting (e.g. a childminder or larger crèche/pre-school), toilets for children may be adult-sized (with training seat and step) or child-sized. Regulation requirements need to be met as regards position of toilet facilities, number of toilets, hand basins, soap and hand drying facilities in all settings. In addition to these requirements, settings should have toilet training and toileting policies and routines worked out so that children work towards independence in a *relaxed, safe and hygienic way*. Policies and routines should consider the following:

- Terminology used in the setting should be decided upon, e.g. wee and poo.
- Children should be prepared for toilet training. Talk about children's body functions. For example, before changing a child's nappy, ask them: 'Did you do poos this time?'
- There are storybooks that deal with the topic of toilet training, e.g. *On Your Potty* by Virgina Miller.
- Staff should look out for signs that a child is ready for toilet training, e.g. hopping up and down, holding their pants in the groin area, having longer dry spells, showing signs of being uncomfortable in a wet or soiled nappy, being able to tell when their nappy is wet or soiled, going to a quiet area while passing faeces, etc.
- Liaise closely with parents with regards to a toilet training plan.
- Ask parents to dress children in easily managed clothes, so children can pull pants up and down easily.
- Some settings establish a routine whereby children sit on the toilet or potty at set intervals. Others believe that this is not necessary and that children will soon learn themselves to identify when they need to toilet and should be allowed to do this naturally.
- Allow children a degree of independence but do not leave them on their own. Young children need to be wiped (from front to back – wearing disposable gloves).
- Children need to be shown a very clear and easily understood hand washing routine and this should be adhered to at all times.

Accidents

Accident Prevention

While Standard 20 of the National Standards for Pre-School Services 2010 specifically addresses the issue of safety and accident prevention (as does Regulation 27 of the Child Care (Pre-School) Regulations 2006), other standards and regulations also have relevance to accident prevention.

- Standard 5, Regulation 8 (organisation and management): Adult–child ratios need to facilitate proper supervision of children.
- Standard 10, Regulation 10 (behaviour): Children's behaviour needs to be closely monitored so that children do not injure each other.
- Standard 13, Regulation 26 (food and drink): Children are not permitted to enter food preparation areas.
- Standard 17, Regulation 18 (premises): Premises are safe secure and suitable for purpose.
- Standard 18, Regulation 28 (facilities): Criteria relating to sleep facilities are particularly important. Temperature should be controlled (16–20°C).
- Standard 10, Regulation 25 (equipment and materials): These must be of suitable design, good repair, non-toxic and conform to safety standards, free from rough edges, sharp corners, pinch and crush points, splinters, exposed bolts or nails.

Example of Outcome and Criteria

Standard 20: Safety

Outcome

Children have their needs met in a safe environment.

Criteria

20.1 There is a positive health and safety culture within the setting, and all necessary precautions are taken to prevent accidents and incidents.

20.2 Children attending the service are supervised at all times.

20.3 Staff members are familiar with relevant health and safety legislation.

20.4 A risk assessment in relation to hazards identified on the premises, both indoors and outdoors, is carried out. Where elimination of any identified hazard is not reasonably practicable, the risk from the hazard must be minimised to a safe level.

20.5 The risk assessment is periodically reviewed, with particular reference to the service's incident and accident records, and to any changes in the service or work practices.

20.6 The premises and outside play area are secure. Children cannot leave the premises unsupervised.

20.7 The indoor and outdoor play areas should provide opportunities for challenge to facilitate the children's ability to learn about risk and their own capabilities within safe limits.

20.8 A written policy is in place in relation to the safe conduct of any outings, to ensure the health, safety and welfare of the participating children.

(National Standards for Pre-School Services 2010: 33)

Regulation 27: Safety Measures

Regulation 27 safety measures include the following.

- Heat-emitting surfaces are protected by a fixed guard or are thermostatically controlled to ensure a safe temperature.
- Hot water is thermostatically controlled.
- Gardens or external play areas are properly fenced and gates secured.
- Hazardous areas are properly fenced off.

(Child Care (Pre-School) Regulations 2006: 66)

Dealing with Accidents

Despite adherence to health and safety measures, accidents can and do occur in settings. Staff need to be able to administer first aid (see below) and also know when and how to summon medical assistance. Regulation 7 (medical assistance) states that pre-school services must ensure that 'adequate arrangements are in place to summon medical assistance promptly in an emergency'. Relevant phone numbers should be prominently displayed.

First Aid

Regulation 6 of the Child Care (Pre-School) Regulations 2006 deals with first aid and first aid boxes.

- Medicines, sprays and lotions should not be stored in first aid boxes. They should be stored separately.
- All medicines should be kept out of the reach of children and should be clearly labelled in their original containers.
- A first aid box should be safely stored in an easily accessible and conspicuous location.

Recommended contents of a first aid box			
Materials	Quantity		
	1–5 children	6–25 children	26–50 children
Hypoallergenic plasters	12	20	20
Sterile eye pads (bandage attached)	2	6	6
Individually wrapped triangular bandages	2	6	6
Small individually wrapped sterile un-medicated wound dressings	1	2	4
Individually wrapped antiseptic wipes	8	8	10
Paramedic shears	1	1	1
Latex gloves – non-powdered latex or Nitril gloves (latex free)	1 box	1 box	1 box
Sterile eye wash	1	2	2

A person trained in first aid for children should be on the premises at all times. Additional trained persons will be required, depending on the extent of the services. A person with first aid training should accompany children on outings. In reality most settings require that all staff have up-to-date recognised first aid qualifications.

Spillages

How spillages are dealt with will depend on their nature. All spillages should be cleaned up as soon as they occur to prevent slipping accidents and infection. Non-hazardous spillages (e.g. spilled juice) can be mopped up using a mop and hot soapy water. The area should be cordoned off until fully dry to prevent slipping accidents. Hazardous spillages (e.g. vomit) need to be treated safely. Staff should wear protective gloves and use paper towels to soak up hazardous waste. Towels need to be disposed of safely in sealed bags and then placed in covered bins. Areas then need to be washed thoroughly using hot soapy water and then with water mixed with a disinfectant.

Safe Play Environment

In providing a safe play environment for children, many points must be considered.
■ Play spaces need to be properly secured (e.g. fenced in).
■ Equipment must be of suitable design and in good repair, conform to safety standards and be free from rough edges, sharp corners, pinch and crush points, splinters, exposed bolts or nails.
■ Materials and resources need to be non-toxic and they must have no small parts if they are given to children aged 0–3.

Adequate Adult Supervision

The childcare regulations recommend the following adult to child ratios to ensure adequate supervision.

Recommended adult–child ratios	
Full/part-time day care services	
Age range	Ratio
0–1 year	1:3
1-2 years	1:5
2-3 years	1:6
3-6 years	1:8

Sessional pre-school services	
Age range	**Ratio**
0–1 year	1:3
1–2½ years	1:5
2½–6 years	1:10

Food Hygiene

As a result of strict food and drink regulations, many settings no longer supply meals to children in their care. This requires parents to supply packed lunches or meals for reheating, with the setting supplying only drinks and snacks. Other settings who may not have adequate food preparation facilities employ outside caterers to supply main meals. If settings wish to supply meals, there are strict regulations that must be followed.

Regulation 26 of the Child Care (Pre-School) Regulations relates to this area.

If settings are to provide food and drink, they must have:

- Adequate and suitable facilities for storage, preparation, cooking and serving of food
- Adequate and suitable eating utensils, hand washing, washing up and sterilising facilities.

Pre-schools are subject to all the same legislation as other food operations, e.g. the Food Hygiene Regulations 1950–1989 and the European Communities (Hygiene and Foodstuffs) Regulations 2000. Both of these pieces of legislation require that food is prepared in a hygienic way in a suitable facility. Staff must be trained in food safety. Training will be based on the food safety management system called HACCP: Hazard Analysis and Critical Control Point.

HACCP

HACCP is a system that enables us to identify and control any hazards that could pose a danger to the preparation of safe food. It involves identifying what can go wrong, planning to prevent this and ensuring that these plans are followed through. The Food Safety Authority of Ireland (FSAI) has produced a pack called 'Safe Catering – Your Guide to Making Food Safely'; this pack should be obtained by any pre-school serving food. It is available to buy and it costs approximately €70, including postage and packing. Among other things, the pack contains the HACCP workbook, a set of record books and an explanatory DVD.

Principles of HACCP

There are seven principles of HACCP, which are outlined below.

1   **Identify the hazards**

    Look at each step (e.g. purchasing, delivery, storage, preparation, cooking, chilling etc.) in your operation and identify what can go wrong. For example, salmonella in a cooked chicken product can be caused by cross-contamination with raw meat (biological hazard).

2   **Determine the critical control points (CCPs)**

    Identify the points in your operation that ensure control of the hazards, e.g. cooking raw meat thoroughly will kill pathogens such as E.coli O167.

3   **Establish critical limit(s)**

    Set limits to enable you to identify when a CCP is out of control, e.g. when cooking beef burgers, the centre of the burger must reach a minimum temperature of 75°C to ensure pathogens are destroyed.

4   **Establish a system to monitor control of the CCP**

    When CCPs and critical limits have been identified it is important to have a way to monitor and record what is happening at each CCP. Monitoring should in all cases be simple, clear and easy to do, e.g. probe refrigerated food to ensure that it is being maintained below 5°C.

5   **Establish the corrective action to be taken when monitoring indicates that a particular CCP is not under control**

    When monitoring indicates that a CCP is not under control, corrective action must be taken, e.g. the temperature of the food in a refrigerator rises to 10°C due to a technical fault. Discard the food and repair the refrigerator using the manufacturer's instructions to ensure the correct temperature of 5°C is achieved.

6   **Establish procedures for verification to confirm the HACCP system is working effectively**

    Review and correct the system periodically and whenever you make changes to your operation, e.g. when replacing an oven verify that the time/temperature settings in the new oven achieves the minimum safe cooking temperature for a particular dish by probing the food.

7   **Establish documentation concerning all procedures and records appropriate to these principles and their application**

    For the successful implementation of HACCP, appropriate documentation and records must be kept and be readily available.

                                                    (Food Safety Authority of Ireland 2009)

Arrivals and Departures

The arrival and departure times of all *staff members* should be recorded both at the beginning and end of the working day and at break times.

Arrival of Children

It should be encouraged that children arrive at the same time each day (if possible) so that they can establish a secure and familiar routine. Some settings operate a rota for managing arrivals. The staff member should greet parents warmly. Give parents an opportunity to inform the setting if there is any information that needs to be passed on, e.g. if the child hasn't eaten anything yet on that particular day. Children (if they are old enough) should be encouraged to hang up their own coats and put their bags into their own cubbyholes before joining the session. Their name should be marked in on the relevant attendance register; some settings also record time of arrival. The child should then be escorted to their room.

When children first come to a setting, there may be a period of separation anxiety. While settings will have a general policy for dealing with this, what actually happens will be different from child to child. Usually, children can come on a few short visits (e.g. 1–2 hours). They may be encouraged to bring a favourite toy from home. Some settings ask parents to stay for the full time on the first visit. Pre-school staff will already have found out as part of the enrolment process what activities the child likes most, so they will be given the opportunity to do some of their favourite things. Explain to the other children in the setting (if they are old enough) that a new child will be joining them and ask the children to make the new child feel welcome.

Staff should explain to parents that while children often settle right in, there can still be tears; this is quite normal. Usually, parents are asked to depart quite quickly: if they stay around too long, the child will pick up on their anxiety and this in itself can upset them. Parents are normally asked to say goodbye and explain to the child that they will be back later, e.g. they have to go to work.

If the child gets upset, staff will work hard to find something that calms the child. If a child does not settle after an extended period, the parent may have to be called and the child brought back the next day to try again.

Departure of Children

Regulation 13 of the Child Care (Pre-School) Regulations 2006 state that when a child is registered with a pre-school service a record must be obtained regarding the name(s) of people authorised to collect the child. If there are changes (i.e. the removal or addition of another person), the setting must be informed in person. Settings should not accept a phone call on the day because of the risk that the person making the phone call is not genuine. Some settings have one or two nominated staff members dealing with departures each day. These staff members are familiar with all parents and they will, therefore, be aware if there is any change to arrangements. A report of each child's day should be given. This may be verbal or, in the case of younger children, a copy of the feeding, sleeping and nappy changing schedule can be given. Time of departure should be noted and initialled.

Anti-bullying

Anti-bullying procedures must take account of two aspects:
- Prevention of bullying
- Dealing with cases of bullying.

Prevention of Bullying

The best way of preventing bullying in any setting is to encourage an atmosphere of mutual respect. Children must receive positive guidance and encouragement towards acceptable behaviour. Staff must never themselves use negative behavioural management techniques, such as shouting at a child, telling them they are bold or naughty or excluding them (e.g. putting them on the naughty chair or mat). Instead, discipline should always be approached from a care perspective.

Here is an example of a scenario where discipline is approached from a care perspective.

- Child A is playing with two wooden trains. Child B comes over and pulls them from Child A. Child A tries to get the trains back and Child B hits him over the head with one of them. Child A begins to cry.
- The practitioner comes over to the children and takes Child B aside, but does not remove him from the group.
- The practitioner kneels down to Child B's level, so that they can communicate clearly with the child.
- The practitioner explains to Child B that what he did really hurt Child A.
- The practitioner patiently asks Child B why he took the trains from Child A.
- Child B will usually say that he wanted to play with the trains.
- The practitioner asks Child B what other way he could have done things. The practitioner guides Child B into coming up with the idea that he could have waited until Child A was finished with the train and then he could have played with the trains himself.
- Once Child B is clear about the idea, the practitioner asks him to repeat the rule and the new way of doing things.
- The practitioner asks Child B to apologise to Child A.

In addition to this caring approach to discipline, children must be informed about what bullying is. Children must be taught that bullying occurs when a child (or group of children) say nasty things, hit, kick, threatened or ignore another child.

There are a number of storybooks that are useful for teaching pre-school children about the issue of bullying.

- *The Juicebox Bully* by Bob Sornson and Maria Dismondy
- *Bullybeans* by Julia Cook
- *Stand Tall Molly Lou Mellon* by Patty Lovel
- *Simon's Hook* by Karen Gedig Burnett and Laurie Barrows.

If practitioners think that these books are too complex for younger children, they can create simple story boards. These can be used to discuss the issue of bullying with the children and to explore what can be done if bullying occurs.

Dealing with Cases of Bullying

Every setting should have a written policy on behaviour management, including dealing with bullying behaviour. As children are very closely supervised and adult–child ratios are low in pre-school settings, incidents of bullying behaviour are usually observed by staff. If it is felt that a particular child is bullying another child or other children, an event sample observation or a series of them must be carried out to see what is actually happening. During the event sample observation, staff (other than the observer) should intervene in the usual way to stop bullying behaviour.

Below is a section of an event sample. The child being observed (TC) is viewed by staff as being constantly involved in disagreements with other children. The purpose of the observation is to objectively observe and document over the course of one day what is the nature of these disagreements. The observation should show whether or not the disagreements are provoked by the other children and also how staff respond to the disagreements.

Time	P/UP	Antecedent	Description of behaviour	Consequence
9.12	UP	Group of four children playing at water tray area.	TC fills small jug with water and begins to drink it. TC then spits out the water at CA. CA yells for room leader.	Room leader comes and asks both children what happened. Room leader explains to TC that spitting is not allowed and takes him away from area. TC has to stay by room leader's side for 10 minutes.
10.34	P	Group of six children sitting at the lunch table, having sandwiches and juice. CC pokes her finger into TC's sandwich.	TC begins pounding CC's sandwich with his fist. CC pushes TC and TC falls backwards.	Room leader hears chair topple and tells TC to sit back up on his chair.
KEY				
P/UP: Provoked/unprovoked				
Antecedent: What happened directly before the behaviour being described				

If an ongoing problem is identified, parents should be informed and an agreed plan (individual learning plan) compiled to help the child change their behaviour. Parents should be asked to reinforce at home what is being said and done in the setting. Parents of the child or children being subjected to bullying behaviour may need to be consulted and the situation explained to them. Staff should clearly explain how the problem is being dealt with and answer any questions parents may have.

Fire/Disaster Plan

Regulation 16 of the Child Care (Pre-School) Regulations 2006 is concerned with fire safety measures. All settings must have a written record of:

- Regular fire drills
- The number, type and maintenance record of fire-fighting equipment and smoke alarms on the premises
- The procedures to be followed in the event of a fire (this procedure must be displayed in a conspicuous position in the premises).

Regulation 27 states that individual heating appliances should not be of the type that has an exposed flame or heating element which could provide an ignition source. (Heaters such as open fires, bar heaters or stand-alone gas heaters are not permitted.)

The principal pieces of legislation governing fire safety are as follows.

- The Fire Services Act 1981
- The Building Control Act 1990, which states that a fire safety certificate is required in respect of most buildings and in cases where buildings (including dwellings) undergo a change of use (e.g. as a pre-school or crèche)
- The Tobacco (Health Promotion and Protection) Regulations 1995, which prohibit consumption of tobacco products in any part of a pre-school, crèche, playgroup, day nursery or other service that caters for pre-school children.

The Department for the Environment and Local Government produced a guide called 'Fire Safety in Pre-schools' in 2009. All settings should have a copy of this guide and use it when compiling their fire safety policy. Two aspects of the guide are very important for services:

- Fire safety management
- Fire safety features.

Fire Safety Management

A good fire safety management plan should include sections on:

- Preventing outbreaks of fire
- Instructing and training staff on fire prevention and fire safety procedures

■ Emergency procedures and evacuation drills
■ Maintenance of fire protection equipment
■ Maintenance of building services
■ Provision of appropriate furnishings and fittings, including bedding
■ Availability of escape routes
■ Keeping fire safety records.

A summary of each of these is given below. However, settings should obtain the 'Fire Safety in Pre-schools' guide when compiling their policy.

Preventing Outbreaks of Fire

There must be no accumulation of waste and no heating appliances with exposed flames or heating elements. Electrical and gas appliances must be in good working order and must be checked regularly. Upholstered seating must be in good repair and must comply with fire safety standards. Waste receptacles must be non-combustible. Cooking equipment must be used safely, e.g. no deep fat frying. Flammable liquids should not be stored inside. There must be no smoking on the premises.

Staff Training

Staff should receive training (updated as necessary) on fire prevention, emergency procedures and evacuation drills. They must be trained in using fire fighting equipment and in checking fire detecting and alarm equipment. The availability of escape routes must be ensured. Details of staff training should be recorded and kept.

Emergency Procedures and Evacuation Drills

It is essential that staff are able to respond effectively by alerting the fire brigade and evacuating the premises safely and without delay. A fire evacuation plan should be in place and sufficient numbers of staff on the premises at all times to carry out the plan. Evacuation plans need to account for the number and age of the children on the premises and measures must be taken if there are children on the premises with disabilities or if there are sleeping children on the premises. Fire drills should ideally be carried out monthly, where a complete evacuation of the premises occurs. Children should be brought to a designated assembly point in the open air and a roll called. A record of fire drills should be kept, with any observed shortcomings noted and changed. A person and their deputy should be appointed to ring the fire brigade in the event of a real fire. A notice of fire evacuation procedures should be proximately displayed.

Maintenance of Fire Protection Equipment

All fire protection equipment should be in good working order. Visual inspection by a member of staff will determine that the equipment is in place and is ready to use if required. However, equipment such as fire extinguishers and smoke alarms should be thoroughly checked by a competent service company on a regular basis. Records of checks should be kept.

Maintenance of Building Services

Settings should have electrical/gas appliances and central heating systems checked on a regular basis. Records of checks should be kept.

Furnishings and Fittings

Furnishings and fittings should be of a standard that they cannot be ignited easily and do not contribute to the rapid spread of fire. This includes bedding, upholstered furniture, curtains, blinds and floor coverings. Particular care should be taken with decorations and lights around Christmas and other occasions.

Fire resistant label.

Availability of Escape Routes

In the event of a fire or other emergency, children and others on the premises must be able to evacuate the premises quickly and safely. Escape routes need to be clearly indicated and free from obstructions. Doors and gates across escape routes need to be easily opened by an adult; areas around escape routes must not be blocked.

Fire Safety Records

A fire safety register for the premises should be established and maintained. The register should contain a complete record of all fire safety matters on the premises and should be kept up to date and available for inspection if required. It is usual to appoint one member of staff (and their deputy) in charge of fire safety. It is necessary that this person is a full-time member of staff and that they (or their deputy) are on the premises at all times.

Fire Safety Features

This section of the guide gives details of the principal fire safety features that are necessary in a pre-school facility. Should a fire occur, there must be adequate means of escape to enable children and staff to evacuate the premises safely. Fires must be detected at an early stage. Measures must be taken to ensure the restriction of the spread of fire.

Adequate Means of Escape

Every room in the building must have an escape route leading to a place of safety in the open air at ground floor level. Distance of travel to escape routes should be limited. If there are more than 20 children being accommodated in any room, alternative escape routes must exist. If children are being accommodated in upper or basement floors, an alternative escape route must be provided (usually by means of a protected stairway, made of fire resistant material such as metal or concrete). Windows should not be considered a primary escape route. However, habitable rooms should have windows large enough for them to be used if necessary as a secondary escape route. It should also be borne in mind that windows can also present a risk to children and that protection against falling from windows is required. The evacuation of children with disabilities requires special consideration. Additional guidance is provided in a separate section of the guidelines (BS 5588: Part 8: 1988: Code of Practice for Means of Escape for Disabled People).

Available escape routes	Maximum travel distance (metres)	
	Active children	Sleeping children
Single escape route	18m	10m
Alternative routes available	45m	20m

Detecting Fire at an Early Stage

A fire alarm system is required in every premises used for pre-school services, in order to give early warning of an outbreak of fire and to ensure that the escape routes can be safely used. For single-storey premises accommodating 20 children or fewer, self-contained fire alarms are usually sufficient. For larger and more complex premises, more elaborate systems will be needed. The guidelines provide detailed information on alarm specifications (see pp. 16–17 of 'Fire Safety in Pre-schools').

Restricting the Spread of a Fire

There should be a fire alarm unit close to high-risk areas, e.g. kitchen, storerooms and laundry. The principal method of restricting the spread of fire between different parts of a building is for certain floors, walls and doors to have an appropriate level of fire resistance. The minimum resistance time is usually 30 minutes, but this may be higher. As mentioned earlier, an important part of fire safety involves the regular servicing of electrical and gas appliances, wiring and heating systems, etc.

Safety Statement

Under the Safety, Health and Welfare at Work Act 2005 all employers have a specific duty to prepare a written safety statement for their business. A safety statement identifies all the potential hazards that exist in a particular place of work and how to best deal with them so that accidents or illness are less likely to occur. While safety statements are unique to each place of work, most pre-schools will have a lot of similar items identified (many of which have been considered in the sections above). One member of staff is usually responsible for reviewing and updating the setting's safety statement.

Planning and Programming

Careful planning and programming must be implemented in several crucial areas, including:

■   Children's rights (see pp. 19–29)
■   Equal opportunities (see Chapter 3)
■   Admissions
■   Key person
■   Behaviour guidance and discipline
■   Supporting transitions
■   Outings and excursions
■   Effective record keeping.

Admissions

Most settings will have an admissions policy and admissions procedures.

Admissions Policy

Here is an example of an admissions policy for an E.C.E.C. setting:

> It is the policy of our childcare service to offer equal access to all children. We welcome all children irrespective of special need, family structure, culture, religion or membership of an ethnic group or minority group.

Admissions Procedures

■   Each child must be at least one year old when formally enrolled at the service.
■   Parents seeking to secure a place for their child must complete an enrolment form.
■   A completed enrolment form much be lodged with the service prior to the child attending the service.
■   Children will be admitted on a first-come-first-served basis, following submission of the enrolment form.
■   If there are no remaining places in the appropriate age group, a waiting list will be drawn up.

- Sometimes admissions policies and procedures are more restricted, e.g. a community crèche serving a socially disadvantaged community may require children from that community only to attend.

Key Person

It is good practice for children's emotional security and for continuity of care and educational provision that each child (particularly children aged 0–3) have a key person or worker. A key person has special responsibility for a set number of children. When children first attend the setting, parents and their children will be introduced to their key worker. The names of children and their key worker may be displayed on a notice board in the entrance area. A key person will ensure that their designated children's needs are recognised and met each day.

The key worker will have many duties. They will:

- Help a child settle in when they first arrive
- Pay particular attention to how the child is settling during the first couple of weeks
- Do the feeding and changing routines of the child as often as possible
- Talk with the parents about their child
- Assist the child to integrate into the group as necessary
- Provide emotional support to the child
- Work with parents to ensure that race, culture, religion, language and family values are being met
- Observe, record and monitor the child's progress
- Encourage parents to participate in their child's development
- Provide feedback and information to parents
- Provide feedback and information to colleagues
- Foster good relationships between the child and the other practitioners in the setting.

Behaviour Guidance and Discipline

Regulation 9 of the Child Care (Pre-School) Regulations 2006 and Standard 10 of the National Standards for Pre-School Services 2010 both address the issue of behaviour management. No corporal, disrespectful, degrading, exploitive, intimidating or harmful punishments are to be used. Children should not be excluded, ignored, neglected or isolated. A written policy regarding behaviour management must be developed, and this should be given to parents.

> Children receive positive guidance and encouragement towards acceptable behaviour, and are supported in finding solutions to problems.
> (National Standards for Pre-School Services 2010: 18)

Effective behaviour management is a complex issue and depends on a number of factors:

■ Quality of the adult–child relationship
■ Forms of discipline
■ Being proactive.

Quality of the Adult–Child Relationship

The quality of the adult–child relationship is very important. Children who feel secure and confident in their relationship with their carer are much more likely to engage with them and respond to their moral guidance. Children can pick up very quickly on negative attitudes and body language. Childcare practitioners, therefore, need to really enjoy their work in order to successfully relate to the children in their care.

Forms of Discipline

The form of discipline used by adults is also very important. Hoffman (1970) identified three different discipline techniques. (Only one of these techniques is acceptable in the childcare setting.)

■ **Love Withdrawal**
   With this technique, the adult withholds attention or love from the child. This is done through isolating the child (putting them on the naughty chair), refusing to talk to the child or saying to the child: 'I don't like you when you do that.'

■ **Power Assertion**
   The adult tries to gain control over the child and the child's resources. This is done through slapping or removing privileges.

■ **Induction**
   The adult uses reasoning and explains the consequences of the child's actions to the child, e.g. 'Don't hit him: he didn't mean to bump into you.'

Of the three techniques, *induction* is seen to be most effective and it is the only one that is acceptable in the ECEC setting. With love withdrawal and power assertion methods, the child is likely to be highly anxious and aroused, thinking more about the punishment than the lesson behind it. With induction, the child is calm and more likely to take on board the reasoning behind what is being said.

Being Proactive

Being proactive means preventing misbehaviour before it takes place. With younger children this may mean removing them from the situation or distracting them. Careful planning is also very closely linked to this, e.g. having enough resources in the setting will mean that children do not end up fighting over the resources.

In addition, it is important that pre-schools and schools advocate a *care perspective* for the promotion of moral development. Such a perspective concentrates on educating children about the importance of engaging in pro-social behaviours, e.g. considering the feelings of others, being sensitive to the needs of others and helping each other.

Supporting Transitions

Throughout their pre-school years, children will make a number of important transitions, e.g. from home to crèche, from the baby room to wobbler room, from wobbler room to toddler room, from toddler room to pre-school, from pre-school to primary school. Stress caused by these transitions can be minimised if the transitions are properly managed. Children are stressed by transitions because of uncertainty and the insecurity that it brings. Jean Piaget believed this to be a normal part of development and used the terms *equilibrium* and *disequilibrium* to describe it.

Equilibrium and Disequilibrium

When a child (or indeed an adult) is exposed to something new about the world that conflicts with their existing ideas, they experience disequilibrium (lack of balance). This can be seen in the example of a child attending primary school for the first time. Disequilibrium is caused by their new environment: big rooms, new faces, lots of children, unfamiliar teachers, school uniforms, packed lunches, books, schoolbags, etc. This causes stress because the child is desperately trying to understand their new environment. Some children will be more stressed by this than others. This just reflects differences in personality and previous life experiences. The child will spend the first few days learning about their new environment, gradually restoring equilibrium. All human beings are motivated to seek equilibrium.

Once this concept is understood, practitioners can help to make transitions less stressful for children. The principal way of doing this is by *familiarisation*. Children can be familiarised with aspects of their new environment before they have to make the transition for real. This reduces disequilibrium and the stress that goes with it. For example, many pre-schools arrange a number of visits to the local primary school for children before they make this transition. This allows the children to become familiar with their surroundings and their new teacher.

Another technique that can be used is something of a reversal of this process. Children bring something familiar from their old environment into their new environment. For example, a toddler starting crèche could bring a toy from home as a comfort object.

Outings and Excursions

Regulation 27 (safety measures) of the Child Care (Pre-School) Regulations 2006 and Standard 20 (safety) of the National Standards for Pre-School Services 2010 both require that a written policy and operational procedures are in place in relation to the safe conduct of outings and excursions. The importance of this cannot be overemphasised. Fortunately, it is a very rare occurance that children come to harm while on outings and excursions. However, when a tragedy does occur, it emphasises the absolute necessity for staff to have failsafe procedures and to follow them exactly.

An outing is normally described as something that is done with children regularly, e.g. visit the local library or local playground. An excursion is something that is done less frequently, e.g. a visit to the zoo or the fire station. While each setting will come up with their own policy and procedures regarding outings and excursions, the following points should be considered.

- Excursions and outings away from the pre-school setting are a valuable and interesting part of the lives of children.
- Excursions and outings must adhere to all safety requirements.
- On enrolment, parents sign a general consent form for a number of named regular outings.
- A risk assessment of any proposed excursion must be carried out during the planning stage and a decision made on whether to proceed.

- Prior written permission will be obtained from parents before children are taken on any other excursions. Details of the excursion, including departure and return times, must be given. Mobile contact details must be given so that staff can be contacted while on the excursion.
- Staff on excursions must be contactable by parents at all times. Mobile phones must be on and answered as soon as it is safe to do so.
- Staff must bring a first aid box on all outings and excursions, together with any other necessary medication (e.g. asthma medication).
- There must be a qualified first aider on all excursions.
- Adult–child ratios must be at least that required by the Child Care (Pre-School) Regulations 2006 – more if the nature of the excursion demands it.
- Each staff member is given absolute responsibility for a nominated number of children.
- An attendance roll is kept and checked after any transitions, e.g. moving from one part of the zoo to another.

Effective Record Keeping

Nowadays there is greater emphasis on record keeping in the pre-school setting. This is necessary to ensure a safe, high-quality service. Any system of record keeping must incorporate the Freedom of Information Acts 1997 and 2003 and the Data Protection Acts 1998 and 2003.

There are two types of records which must be kept in settings:

- Operational records
- Child-related records.

Operational Records

Operational records are records demonstrating compliance with the Child Care (Pre-School) Regulations 2006, National Standards for Pre-School Services 2010, Aistear, Síolta and all the relevant legislation detailed earlier in this chapter. This can be a very daunting task. However, if settings have a good system of record keeping, they can approach this very sizable piece of work in a systematic fashion.

Some relevant points to consider are listed below.

- Before a setting will be permitted to open at all, they will have to demonstrate to HSE inspectors that they have a system of all the essential operational records in place.
- Settings can design an effective system of filing and storage, e.g. an arch lever file for master copies of all policies and procedures.
- Settings should have a strong metal fireproof filing cabinet for all sensitive or confidential information.
- In drafting operational records, prioritise the work to be carried out. Work through the list of operational records bit by bit.

Child-related Records

Depending on the nature of the information, child-related records may be stored in various ways.

Central Files

Files containing certain types of information about children need to be kept in a secure location in the setting. It is advisable to have an office in the setting with a lockable fireproof filing cabinet for this purpose. Information such as parents' names and contact details, medical information or copies of reports from other professionals (e.g. physiotherapists) are usually stored in individual files and alphabetically arranged in the cabinet.

It is important that, while this information is securely kept, staff working with the child have access to the information if required. In addition to physical, paper-based information, settings may have information stored electronically on computer. Computers should be password protected.

Learning Portfolios

Each child in the setting should have an individual learning portfolio in which selected samples of their work are stored. Portfolios can take the form of a folder, scrapbook or box. Children should be involved in decisions about what goes into their learning portfolio: this will encourage them to think about the quality of the work they are producing and the amount of effort they are putting into it. Photographs can be taken of larger pieces of work or of activities that do not have an end product and these photographs can be included in the learning portfolio, with captions.

Practitioner Files

In most settings, children have one key worker. Key workers should have a practitioner file for every child assigned to them. This may take the form of one big arch lever file with coloured dividers separating each child's information. Information such as observation notes and records, attendance and records of conversations with parents or other staff members about the child can be kept here. Information in practitioner files may be transferred to the central file at the end of the year.

Staffing Policies
Staff Ratios

Regulation 8 (management and staffing) of the Child Care (Pre-School) Regulations 2006 deals with the issue of staff ratios. While staff–child ratios given in the guidelines are based on age group, the regulation also emphasise the importance of having mixed age groupings or allowing siblings from different age groups to interact. In this way, although staff ratios are given per age group in the regulations, the total number of childcare staff available in the setting should be considered, as opposed to the 'per room' ratio only.

Full day care		Part-time day care		Sessional pre-school		Temporary drop-in centres		Overnight	
Age	Ratio	Age	Ratio	Age	Ratio	Age	Ratio	Age	Ratio
0–1 year	1:3	0–1 year	1:3	0–1 year	1:3	0–6 years	1:4	0–1 year	1:3
1–2 years	1:5	1–2 years	1:5	1–2½ years	1:5	• Max group size: 24		1–6 years	1:5
2–3 years	1:6	2–3 years	1:6	2½ –6 years	1:10	• No more than two children under 15 months per adult			
2½ –6 years	1:10	3–6 years	1:8						

Communication

While being respectful of the need for confidentiality, information relevant to children's welfare and development needs to be shared with relevant staff. Managers of settings need to make time for meeting with their staff one-to-one to discuss any necessary issues. This should be done on a regular basis and is sometimes called 'staff supervision' or 'staff support'. In larger settings, lunchtimes are often staggered, so staff members may have little time to meet or interact. An effort must be made for regular staff meetings and an agenda should be posted in advance of the meeting so that additional issues can be added. The meeting should be chaired by the childcare manager and minutes taken for future reference. In larger settings, staff notice boards are useful, as is staff email and texting. Prior to any policy or procedure being finalised, staff should be consulted and their views should be taken on board.

Staff Training and Development

ECEC services in Ireland are currently working towards having all staff qualified to Early Childhood Education and Care Level 5 at least. Some settings are contributing financially for their staff to complete qualifications at night, while still working during the day. There are increasingly large numbers of practitioners with higher qualifications than that: QQI Level 6 and also Level 7 and 8 degrees. This is certainly a good thing for increasing quality of provision. In countries like New Zealand, ECEC services are predominantly graduate led. Apart from initial training, ECEC practitioners benefit greatly from ongoing in-service training. Private providers, voluntary groups, CCCs and local VECs often provide training relevant to the ECEC sector. ECEC practitioners are required to keep their first aid training up to date. A record of all in-service training should be maintained.

Staff Illness

There are two important issues in relation to staff illness: (1) illness prevention and (2) dealing with staff absences. In terms of illness prevention, all staff should have up-to-date immunisations. Illness and exclusion policies for children in the setting need to be enforced in order to protect staff (and other children in the setting) from infections. Good hygiene routines also need to be in place for the same reason. Stress and low morale can contribute to staff illness. It is important that settings acknowledge this and take measures to prevent either becoming an issue. Physical environment, pay and conditions all contribute to how well a setting will function. Every effort should be made to create a bright, clean, well-resourced working environment. Staff should have pay and working conditions that reflect the important role they play in children's wellbeing and development.

If a staff member does become ill and needs to be absent from the setting, a set procedure should be followed so that a contingency plan can be put in place for the duration of their absence. Procedures can include some of the following aspects.

- The staff member should phone the centre manager as soon as they know they will be absent.
- If possible, the staff member gives an indication of how long they will be absent, so that the manager can act accordingly.
- Some larger settings have a 'floating' member of staff, who covers for absences as required.
- Sometimes settings in an area maintain a list of Garda-vetted, part-time staff. These part-time workers can be called upon for staff absences of more than a day or so.
- If the setting is providing work placement for Level 6 students (who have already completed Level 5), with the permission of their college they may be offered temporary work to cover staff absences.

Confidentiality

At all times the issue of confidentiality must be considered in the ECEC setting. Issues that arise should never be the subject of general conversation outside the setting. Sometimes, as part of a student's coursework, they may be required to give examples from their work experience. If this is the case, the name of the setting and the names of the children concerned should be protected. Sensitive information about children and their families is usually shared with the child's key worker. Usually, other members of staff are given this information on a need-to-know basis only. Records should be kept in a locked but accessible fireproof filing cabinet and/or on a password protected computer system.

Equality and Diversity in ECEC

Introduction to Equality and Diversity

When we speak of equality and diversity, we are referring to the concept of having respect for people, e.g. respecting their identity and their beliefs.

> **Equality** refers to 'the importance of recognising different individual needs and of ensuring equity in terms of access, participation and benefits for all children and their families.
>
> **Diversity** refers to 'the diverse nature of Irish society for example in terms of social class, gender, returned Irish emigrants, family status, minority groups and the majority group.
>
> (National Childcare Strategy 2006–2010 Diversity and Equality Guidelines for Childcare Providers: vi)

Ireland at one time was not aware of the many minority groups we know today. Even if there was an awareness of minority groups, diversity may not have been truly valued in Irish society. As a result of the demographic change in Ireland in recent times and the rise of various minority groups, diversity issues have come to the fore. The Celtic Tiger period of Irish society played a part in this: when there was no shortage of jobs, Ireland was an attractive place for people of different nationalities to come to work.

Diversity can be a very positive thing, if people become familiar with, learn about and embrace difference cultures. Unfortunately, diversity sometimes brings prejudice and conflict. Diversity can cause some people anguish, since different people can react differently when they encounter people from minority groups.

According to the National Childcare Strategy 2006–2010 Diversity and Equality Guidelines for Childcare Providers (CMC 2006: vi) the term 'minority group' includes but is not limited to:

- People with a disability
- The Traveller community
- Economic migrants
- Black Irish
- Irish-language speakers
- Refugees
- Asylum seekers
- Children with gay or lesbian parents
- Families of minority religious faith.

Under the Equal Status Acts 2000–2004, discrimination is prohibited on nine grounds:

- Gender
- Marital status
- Family status
- Sexual orientation
- Religious belief
- Age
- Disability
- Race
- Membership of the Traveller community.

As a result of the multifaceted population in Ireland, practitioners work with children from minority groups and it is their task to ensure that they are integrated well into education and all children are treated equally.

Equality and Diversity is just as important in childhood as the concept is in adulthood and included in many childcare documents to ensure best practice. The National Children's Strategy identifies educational diversity in childhood as an objective:

> Children will be educated and supported to value social and cultural diversity so that all children including travellers and other marginalised groups achieve their full potential. (DoHC 2000: 70)

Equality and diversity are also linked to Aistear.

> Promoting equality is about creating a society which provides equal opportunities for everyone and gives people the freedom to reach their full potential.
> Promoting diversity is about welcoming and valuing individual and group differences, and understanding and celebrating difference as a part of life.
> (NCCA 2009: 8)

Aistear makes the following points in relation to equality and diversity.

- All children are unique and each has different traits and qualities: no two children are exactly the same. Children can come from many different backgroundsand cultures. Each child has a basic right to be treated equally with dignity and respect.
- Adults should be aware of the fact that children can develop bias and prejudice at any age. They are open to how other people think and can be easily influenced; they pick up on other people's opinions regarding race, culture, etc.
- Children should be given opportunities to learn about other cultures of the world and different ways of life as well as their own in order for them to become increasingly aware of diversity.
- Adults and educators should help and encourage children to have respect for different ways of life, other beliefs and cultures and to learn the importance of diversity. They should also do their best to promote diversity in other people such as parents, relations and friends and to challenge discrimination if they think it is happening.

Síolta highlights the fact that equality and diversity are covered under its 12 principles.

- Equality is a very important characteristic of Síolta.
- Síolta emphasises diversity and is concerned that the cultures of minority groups are recognised.

The importance of childhood diversity has been recognised not only in Ireland but also internationally. The United Nations Convention on the Rights of the Child (UNCRC) refers to the principles of diversity and non-discrimination.

> All children and adults have the right to evolve and to develop in a context where there is equity and respect for diversity. Children, parents and educators have the right to good-quality early childhood education services, free from any form of – overt and covert, individual and structural – discrimination due to their race, colour, sex, language, religion, political or other opinion, national, ethnic or social origin, property, disability, birth or other status.
> (Article 2, UNCRC)

Ireland committed to ensuring these rights were in practice when the UNCRC was ratified in 1992. The state proposed to:

> ...take all appropriate measures to ensure that the child is protected against all forms of discrimination or punishment on the basis of the status, activities, expressed opinion, or beliefs of the child's parents, legal guardians, or family members.
> (Article 2, UNCRC)

Equality and Diversity Initiatives in Ireland

Éist

The Éist project was funded under the Equal Opportunities Childcare Programme (EOCP). It came about in recognition of the fact that ECEC settings of the time did not have access to appropriate good-quality training or even useful resources in relation to equality and diversity. It also highlighted the need for practitioners to engage in personal reflection and anti-discrimination work. The project lasted for three years and it raised awareness about the need for an organised and appropriate equality and diversity training approach that was particularly geared towards ECEC. This training approach has been put into practice and tested across the ECEC sector.

The Éist project, which worked closely with CCCs, was responsible for promoting the inclusion of diversity, equality and anti-racism issues at policy level. It formulated equality guidelines for ECEC educators. Éist also worked at international level in conjunction with the Diversity in Early Childhood Education and Training (DECET) network. DECET includes a number of European organisations with common goals regarding the value of equality and diversity in ECEC (see p. 136).

Éist introduced a training manual entitled 'Ar an mBealach', meaning 'On the Way'. The aim of 'Ar an mBealach' was to ensure the implementation of an equality and diversity training programme for the ECEC sector that would be of the highest quality. The manual relates particularly to Ireland and it highlights important issues for the educator and for the child, e.g. racism and discrimination.

Pre-school Education Initiative for Children from Minority Groups

This project, which began in 2011 and is now complete, was led by EdeNn, Clare County Childcare Committee and Cork City Childcare Committee. The project aimed to provide support to children from minority groups in an ECEC setting.

The FETAC (Level 5) module on Equality & Diversity in Childcare was delivered nationwide. ECECD staff were involved in a mentoring programme and a DVD was produced as a result of the initiative. Participants learned about the anti-bias approach and how to implement it. The initiative was deemed successful and it was the first time such an initiative was delivered at a national level.

The Role of the Practitioner

Practitioners play a very significant role in educating children regarding equality and diversity. As part of their job, they will meet, care for and educate children from different diversities, e.g. different countries, ethnic origins and family structures.

Practitioners must ensure that they welcome all children equally and value such diversity. They must recognise and appreciate that families have different beliefs, ideas and approaches to situations. They must strive to enable children to understand the meaning of diversity, mix with other children from diverse backgrounds and be introduced to their cultures and values. Children that welcome diversity at an early age can often have a greater capacity to socialise when they become adults.

Young children are highly influenced by adults. Therefore, practitioners must ensure that they are aware of their own attitudes and experiences and how these can affect their professional role. Practitioners must not show any negativity or bias regarding diversity around children, since children can pick up on this. Children can also adopt prejudices and negative feelings to minority groups from parents.

The practitioner must ensure that they show an awareness of diversity in ECEC. They must be very observant of new children from minority backgrounds in their environment. They need to be aware of the possibility that these children may feel isolated. Therefore, practitioners must ensure that all children are invited to participate and given opportunities to mix with one another.

The practitioner must also be observant of any kind of negativity from the other children. This may come about because of a lack of understanding by the children – perhaps they have heard their parents talk about certain groups in a stereotypical way. Practitioners must challenge this negativity. They should ensure that all kind of discrimination or judgments towards other children are dealt with according to policies and procedures relating to the particular education facility.

Practitioners must facilitate children in developing a positive self-identity. They should not have any expectations of children, or label or stereotypes them in any way. For example, all children are free to use games and toys even if they are classed as being for the opposite sex (i.e. boys are allowed to play with the kitchen and girls are allowed to work at the builders' bench).

It is the responsibility of the practitioner to provide a suitable physical environment in which to promote children's learning and development. Children must feel safe and at home; the ECEC environment must be an environment where children can be themselves. Opportunities provided in the environment can help to build each child's individual and group identity and help them to understand difference and what it means to be different. The environment should communicate that diversity is a positive thing and is of great value.

The environment must treat children equally: all children must be given opportunities to work on various exercises and activities. Practitioners must regularly include new and exciting lessons regarding equality and diversity. By providing an environment rich in diversity, settings can help and encourage parents to recognise diversity and minority groups also. Adults and children can see that everyone is equal and can all work together.

Practitioners must ensure that they provide equal opportunities for girls as well as boys in the setting. Quite early on, children are aware of stereotypical roles, e.g. girls play with the kitchen and boys plays with the work bench. Boys can often feel embarrassed to play with 'girls' toys' such as dolls, prams or ironing boards. Practitioners must try their best to provide a gender-positive environment, where both genders have the opportunities to play together on whatever things they choose. No equipment must be perceived as being for a specific gender. The educator can encourage boys and girls to play together by organising joint activities and by putting together toys that might be deemed to be girls' toys and toys that might be deemed to be boys' toys. This can help children to develop a positive identity.

Practitioners must ensure that the environment is inclusive to all children. The classroom must be suitable for the children that will be attending, e.g. the setting must be accessible for wheelchair access. Practitioners must ensure that the play materials and books in the classroom reflect the diversity of the children in attendance. Art materials must be resourced properly so that children can create images of people with many different skin tones. Pieces of equipment must be labelled correctly so that children whose first language is not English can develop their fluency.

Aistear's theme of Identity and Belonging is all about promoting an environment in which children can focus on who they are and feel a sense of belonging. (See p. 81 for more information on Aistear.)

Diversity in Early Childhood Education and Training (DECET)

Diversity in Early Childhood Education and Training (DECET) is a European network that represents organisations working in the field of ECEC in Ireland, Belgium, France, Germany, Greece, the Netherlands, England, Scotland and Spain.

DECET suggests that practitioners should adopt the following principles.

- **Accept diversity in society and do not be judgmental**
  Practitioners should embrace all children and never have any preconceptions based around other cultures.
- **Have an open mind and be open to learning about different cultures and beliefs**
  Practitioners cannot know everything and by keeping an open mind they can learn new things.
- **Show empathy and understanding towards parents and their children**
  Practitioners must see things from other people's points of view.

■ **Be flexible and adaptable to different children's needs**

Children and their families from different diversities may require extra guidance from practitioners; this must be taken into account.

■ **Be sensitive and responsive**

It is important for practitioners to have a sensitive and understanding side; children can pick up on this.

■ **Support a sense of belonging**

Practitioners must help children to establish and be comfortable with who they are.

■ **Be enthusiastic, engaged and motivated**

Being enthusiastic and motivated comes across well to children and provides a very positive environment.

■ **Be creative in order to find alternative solutions and approaches**

Practitioners must always include a range of different activities to suit every child's learning style. Practitioners must give children the freedom to be creative.

■ **Show warmth and be caring towards children**

Practitioners must ensure that the children are the main priority. Practitioners can foster this concept by having an approachable personality.

The National Childcare Strategy

The National Childcare Strategy gives guidelines on promoting equality and diversity in ECEC setting, as follows.

■ Provide CDs of children's songs in a number of different languages. The language will focus on English and Irish but educators can also include different languages from different cultures. Children can listen to them in the classroom on a regular basis. It is surprising how quickly children will pick up on new languages.

■ Allow children regular access to art materials with which they can paint, draw and colour different images that incorporate a range of skin tones. Children can talk about their images when they are finished.

■ Provide toys or images familiar to an individual child so that a sense of belonging is fostered. Items that represent diversity will benefit all children in the ECEC setting (e.g. a sari in the dress-up box).

■ Display pictures of children and their families around the classroom. Pictures should be displayed at the children's level, so that they can see the images whenever they wish. When the children look at such images, there is an opportunity for them to chat about similarities and differences, e.g. family structures, different types of housing, etc.

- Provide a wide range of children's books that show images of diverse people and their lives. Recent books are unlikely to have stereotypical roles seen in books from previous times. Many books will provide pictures of children from minority groups; children will be curious about pictures with other children in them.
- Provide books in languages related to minority groups and books showing sign language and Braille.
- Introduce children to musical instruments from different countries.
- Provide props for dramatic play that reflect the reality of children's home backgrounds, e.g. disability aids, diverse cooking utensils.
- Provide simple cookery lessons during which children can make certain foods related to different countries. They can taste them and discuss similarities and differences from typically Irish foods.

Practitioners from Minority Groups

It is quite common to have a practitioner from the same or similar minority group to children in an ECEC setting, e.g. similar background, ethnicity or disability. This can be a very positive experience for children and can offer good support to parents also. The child can relate to the practitioner and they can be reassured that being a bit different from the other children is not a bad thing. Perhaps if there is a language barrier, the practitioner can be particularly beneficial.

It can be a very positive experience for children in the majority group also. Practitioners will have a vast amount of knowledge and experience to pass on to the children. They can share their knowledge of festivals, customs, different foods and music. Lessons that come from a person who has direct experience of something are always more powerful and authentic.

Approaches to Equality and Diversity

A number of approaches have been identified to develop a curriculum in diversity education. Through these approaches children have opportunities to reach their full potential. The approaches are:

- Multicultural
- Intercultural
- Anti-bias.

Multicultural Approach

Multicultural refers to society, group, school or organisation where people of different ethnicities, cultures and religions live, work and communicate with each other. (Murray 2012: 115)

Through multicultural education, children are encouraged to learn about the beliefs, values and rules of language in their own culture and in the cultures of other children in the ECEC setting. Multicultural education also educates students to be valued citizens, taking other people's views into consideration as well as their own.

Practitioners can do many things to provide a multicultural education. For example, in circle time the practitioner may present a group lesson on a country such as Spain. Maybe a child within the setting was born in Spain or has Spanish parents. The educator can use this to plan and implement a lesson. Materials authentic to Spain are gathered, such as a Spanish flag or a Spanish dress. These items are introduced to the rest of the children and the significance is explained. The children are taught about Spain as a country and they are given interesting facts. The children are also introduced to Spanish food. When the lesson is complete and any questions have been answered, the children can complete an art activity based on Spain.

Activities such as this will integrate all children and will create an interest in different cultures, while also raising the self-esteem of the child connected to the specific culture.

Intercultural Approach

According to the NCCA, intercultural education is:

> ...education which respects, celebrates and recognises the normality of diversity in all areas of human life. It sensitises the learner to the idea that humans have naturally developed a range of different ways of life, customs and worldviews, and that this breadth of human life enriches all of us.
> ...It is education which promotes equality and human rights, challenges unfair discrimination, and promotes the values upon which equality is built.
> (NCCA, 'Intercultural Education in the Primary School': 3)

Through the intercultural approach, children from majority and minority groups have the opportunity to experience other cultures and engage and learn from each other. This promotes awareness and mutual respect. The ability to talk and use language skills is a fundamental component of intercultural education, since adults need to give children accurate information and also challenge any stereotypes or prejudice they may have learned. Best practice is by talking with the child about their thoughts and opinions in a very relaxed manner, instead of lecturing them as to what is wrong and right. This approach is an important part of every child's educational experience and it helps to prepare them for adult life by fostering the necessary skills and attitudes. The approach is suitable for all children, irrespective of their age or ethnicity.

Anti-bias Approach

The anti-bias approach was developed by Louise Derman-Sparks and the Anti-Bias Task Force in the US. It was further developed by Glenda MacNaughton (Melbourne University) and DECET. It provides common goals regarding equality and diversity among young children. This approach is a very active approach which challenges prejudice or bias that people have. Unfortunately, young children can often show negative attitudes towards other children who are different in any way to the 'norms' they are used to. The anti-bias approach promotes diversity and assists children in recognising difference and realising that being different is not a bad thing. Such an approach can facilitate children in developing a healthy positive attitude towards diversity, which will stay with them in later life. Practitioners implement the anti-bias curriculum on a daily basis with the children as well as parents and colleagues in their care.

The anti-bias approach also focuses on addressing inequalities. It helps children to develop a strong self-identity and the strength and determination to stand up for themselves and other people, if necessary.

Anti-bias education reflects the rights enshrined in the UNCRC:

- The right to survival
- The right to develop to the fullest
- The right to protection from harmful influences, abuse, and/or exploitation
- The right to participate fully in family, cultural and social life.

The anti-bias approach also facilitates professionals to ensure that they engage in regular personal reflection in order for them to carefully establish whether or not they need to make any changes to themselves or their settings. As we know, practitioners play a vital role in a child's development and are very much involved in their day-to-day lives. Practitioners can be highly influential and, because of this, they must ensure that they question and explore their own attitudes and ideas regarding equality and diversity. Unfortunately, adults can at times have negative thoughts about issues surrounding diversity. Therefore, an effort must be made to be self-aware. Practitioners must ensure that anything they say or do will not affect children in a negative way. Children can easily pick up messages from adult behaviours, e.g. listening to how adults talk when they do not think that children are listening. Practitioners should always try to improve and be creative by thinking of new activities in relation to diversity issues.

There are three specific goals that relate to the anti-bias approach:

- Developing and supporting children's identities and self-esteem
- Allowing children to feel comfortable with difference
- Helping children to recognise diversity, bias and stereotypes.

Developing and Supporting Children's Identities and Self-esteem

This first goal is in relation to encouraging children to be confident in how they feel within themselves. It helps children to develop a sense of belonging and a comfort in knowing who they are at both individual and group levels. One of the roles of the practitioner is to become familiar with the various different backgrounds of the children and then decide accordingly if every child is individually represented within the setting. Practitioners can implement relevant activities around this goal, e.g. an activity on the children's names and the correct spelling of the names. The classroom environment should reflect different groups in the classroom, e.g. different flags and other items related to different cultures. Practitioners can include diversity lessons relating to children's identities, e.g. sampling different foods, becoming familiar with different dress, etc. The children can be encouraged to talk about their families and to show photographs and then establish the similarities and differences between families. The practitioner designs lessons and activities where children can explore various types of homes and family structures.

Allowing Children to Feel Comfortable with Difference

This goal refers to a child's ability to observe and question various relevant similarities and differences between different people within their environment. The practitioner acts as a guide in helping the children to comprehend these differences.

The professional also takes on the role of observer and establishes how the children interact with each other, how they cope in different situations and, if there are any children being isolated, what might be the reasons for this. Practitioners must ensure that careful observation takes place and that they recognise discrimination and know how to respond appropriately to it.

It is often a good idea to establish a number of 'ground rules' or 'class rules' in the education setting. This can be a very appropriate measure, particularly if the children are given the opportunity to help. The first rule might be that children must only ever call another person by their real name. The reason for this rule should be explained, i.e. if people are not called by their real name, this can hurt their feelings. Some more rules can be identified, e.g. that all people in the setting must be treated nicely and with respect and that everyone must be polite to one another.

If an incident occurs regarding prejudice or discrimination, the practitioner must immediately intervene but they must ensure that they are sensitive at all times. The practitioner can follow up on any incidents as soon as they arise. If a child says or does something hurtful to another child who they class as being 'different', the practitioner will challenge the child about what was said. The practitioner can give accurate information and explanations in language that young children will understand, while also ensuring that the child understands the hurt caused. The child who was hurt will also be supported. The practitioner will act sensitively throughout, taking into consideration the feelings of *both* children. Over time, children can develop the confidence to say such phrases as: 'I don't like you calling me that name.'

Helping Children to Recognise Diversity, Bias and Stereotypes

As children become older, they have an increasing awareness of various comments, ideas and beliefs that can be biased, untrue, inaccurate and hurtful. This goal aims to help children to become critical thinkers and to comprehend what is true/untrue, fair/unfair. Children can also begin to learn skills to resist biases and stereotypes that can influence them.

The role of the practitioner for this goal is to challenge children about stereotypes, should they arise. The practitioner challenges typical stereotypes, e.g. Mammy makes the dinner and Daddy goes to work. The educator can introduce stories and pictures where, for example, Daddy is minding the baby. The practitioner can ask the children to speak about such stereotypes and establish if they are accurate or not. Children will also learn how other people might feel when they come up against such prejudice; through this, children can learn appropriate support skills.

Children can learn so much through an anti-bias curriculum that provides them with exciting and fun experiences in diversity.

Policies on Equality and Diversity

It is especially important that all ECEC settings have the necessary policies and guidelines in place in relation to equality and diversity issues. A policy on equality and diversity is appropriate evidence of the commitment to comply with the Equal Status Acts 2000 to 2004 and the Employment Equality Acts 1998 and 2004. Having a policy on diversity and equality is necessary for practitioners, since it states best practice within ECEC settings. It provides all practitioners with up-to-date information and allows them to become familiar with equality and diversity. They know what is expected of them at all times and they know how discrimination may occur within the setting. The policy may include the views of employees regarding equality and diversity, a detailed explanation of the meaning of stereotyping, knowledge of different cultures and values and effective anti-racism and anti-discrimination practices.

The policy gives parents reassurance and peace of mind that when they are not present, their child is receiving the best possible care by the best-quality practitioners who are knowledgeable on important issues. They know that there are equal opportunities for all children and the setting is dedicated to facilitating them to reach their full potential. They are aware that in the event of any kind of incident occurring, the matter will be dealt with according to policy and in a very professional manner. When a written policy is present, it can be referred to on many occasions and there will be no discrepancies or misunderstandings.

Practitioners and Parents Working Together

Families and practitioners that work in unison can support the development of diversity within the ECEC setting. Parents are the most knowledgeable people when it comes to their children and they can provide information to staff if required on important elements of their culture or values, e.g. different celebrations or appropriate foods. It is important that practitioners communicate effectively with parents so that they can follow the parents' wishes for their child. Practitioners must ensure that they acknowledge and address any queries or concerns of parents. Practitioners and parents must talk and listen to each other, thus promoting respect.

Practitioners must ensure that they are familiar with the exact name of the minority group, i.e. how parents wish to be addressed. They must ensure that they are inclusive of diverse family structures, e.g. one-parent family, foster parents, adoptive parents, etc.

Practitioners may engage parents in short meetings based on equality and diversity, not necessarily for minority groups but also for majority groups. Here any issues can be pointed out in a quiet and relaxed atmosphere, since it is often too busy in the ECEC setting to speak properly with parents on a regular basis. Practitioners can provide information on equality and diversity. They can ensure that parents are familiar with the two terms. Practitioners can examine any policies on equality and diversity and explain in detail the protocol used if any kind of prejudice or discrimination becomes evident and the specific reasons behind it.

All staff must ensure that everything they hear from parents in the ECEC setting remains confidential.

Religion

Religion can be an important part of identity for many families. Practitioners must ensure that they are aware of the specific religions that children may follow. Children cannot choose their religion until they are much older; while they are young, it is the responsibility of parents to make the choice for them.

In Ireland nowadays there are numerous religions. The majority religion in Ireland is Roman Catholic. However, there are also many other religions practised, e.g. Church of Ireland, Jehovah's Witnesses, Buddhist and Jewish. Some children may be brought up to follow two religions because their parents may follow two different religions. Some people do not practise any religion and are known as atheists.

There are many religious traditions that are important in many children's lives and often feature in childcare learning activities. The celebration of traditional festivals can be a very positive and enjoyable experience for children. However, practitioners should consult families about whether or not their child should participate in organised celebrations associated with a religion (especially if it is a religion to which they do not belong). Some parents may not place much of an emphasis on it, whereas other parents will. Topics such as this one should be discussed with parents before the child begins in the ECEC setting; this will ensure that the wishes of parents are respected from the very beginning. Practitioners must explain to parents in advance if a Christian lesson is taking place, e.g. an activity based on Christmas. Parents can then decide if they wish their children to join in. If not, invite parents to suggest alternative activities in which their child can take part.

Practitioners must ensure that every child feels included in the classroom, even if they have a different religion from the other children. Practitioners must have certain knowledge about different religions that children follow; it is not enough for practitioners to be aware of their own religion only. They should not have any prejudice against or make any assumptions about particular religions, they should simply respect them.

No child should ever be excluded because of their faith or religion, nor should they be expected to join in activities that are not consistent with their religion. Article 30 of the UNCRC explains:

> Minority or indigenous children have the right to learn about and practise their own culture, language and religion. The right to practise one's own culture, language and religion applies to everyone.

It may be the policy of the ECEC setting that if a particular festival or celebration is taking place in a minority religion of a child within the setting, this celebration is acknowledged. Perhaps mentioning it in the classroom in a positive way will help the child to feel valued just as much as the children in the majority religion. The child's family will be able to provide plenty of useful information on the celebration.

Practitioners can provide children with some information on different religions and festivals in language that is simple and easy to follow. Practitioners may also introduce a calendar on which important dates relating to religious celebrations are noted. Children can check the calendar every day to see if there is anything significant for that day. In some cases, it may be decided that no religious festivals are celebrated; it may depend on the policy of the particular setting. By doing this, however, children will miss out on many celebrations and practitioners will be unable to avail of many valuable teaching moments.

Practitioners can introduce a variety of books that mention different religious celebrations. There are a wide variety of books at present available from local libraries. These books will have vibrant pictures and terms that are easy to understand.

Practitioners must ensure that they strictly follow guidelines related to the food preferences of certain religions. Parents can help with this at the very beginning of the year to prevent any confusion. Management must ensure that the necessary ingredients are available at all times.

The Childcare Professional

Section 1: The Childcare Professional

Attributes of a Childcare Professional

The childcare professional plays a vital role and has a powerful influence on a child's overall development: cognitive, social, emotional and intellectual. Since the 1990s in particular, Ireland has become much more aware of the value of this influence and the importance of the role of the childcare professional. Childcare professionals are responsible for providing a holistic and safe environment for the children in their care as well as implementing a developmentally appropriate early childhood curriculum, while ensuring it is in accordance with the relevant legislation, policies and procedures. They must ensure children are taught through a curriculum that will allow them to thrive and reach their full potential. The childcare professional can spend a significant amount of time with the same children on a regular basis, e.g. children that attend playschool or Montessori school four mornings a week. Parents place their trust in childcare professionals when they leave their children in their care. As we are aware, working with children is a career choice that is very rewarding. Nevertheless, like all other professions, there can be challenging times. It is clear that there is a need to ensure that all childcare professionals have the necessary qualities and values as well as the necessary qualifications for their role and that they have the ability to provide leadership and guidance to children. The attributes integral to a childcare professional include those listed overleaf.

Respectful

This quality really is a necessity; it is one the basics for anyone who works in the childcare sector. All children and their families must be respected, regardless of social background, culture or religion. Childcare professionals must also respect all colleagues and members of staff. Treating everyone with the utmost respect allows everyone to get on well and work together.

Friendly

The childcare professional must be approachable and cheerful when looking after and educating children. Children should feel at ease around them. Children should feel happy to ask for help or guidance with anything. The same also goes for parents, who should feel that they can approach the childcare professional and can have a chat with them about any concern regarding their child. Childcare professionals must ensure that they do not bring any personal problems into the workplace.

Fair

Childcare professionals must be fair in the manner in which they look after the children. For example, in managing a behaviour issue in which two children are involved in conflict, it is important that both children are spoken to in the same format. A childcare professional has no favourites: all children are treated equally.

Patient

The childcare professional is required to be patient with children at all times. They may have up to ten children in their care at any one time. Children can cry and they can be noisy and demanding. The childcare professional, therefore, should be of a calm nature. They must do their very best not to become stressed or raise their voice.

Organised

Since the childcare professional may have up to ten children in their care at any one time, they must be organised. They must ensure that they have time to prepare the room before the children arrive. All items needed for the day must be prepared and within easy reach. Childcare professionals are required to be consistent and employ a routine so that the children know what way the day runs and what to expect.

Caring

It is important that childcare professionals have a caring, sensitive side. Whatever they do must be in the best interests of the children, taking into account their individual needs. It is also important that the childcare professional is aware and responsive to each child's feelings.

Professional

Childcare professionals are required to act in a professional manner at all times. They must have professional standards; for example, they must not use a mobile phone unless they are on a break and they must not chat socially with colleagues in front of the children. If they do this, it means that they cannot be focused entirely on their work. It is important that practitioners never bring any personal problems into the workplace, since the children are the main priority. Best practice is to build positive relationships with children and their parents and to be friendly towards them, at the same time remembering that they are not family members or friends. Choose language carefully: it is important not to offend parents in any way. The need for confidentiality must also be remembered. Childcare professionals are always aware of confidentiality in the workplace.

Hardworking

The childcare professional is required to be a hard worker. They will most likely work as part of a team and in order for the team to work well and be successful all members must work equally hard. Working in the childcare profession involves many fun activities with the children (e.g. painting and storytelling) but there is so much other important work to be done on a regular basis (e.g. planning lessons and activities, observations and personal reflection).

Punctual

Being punctual is necessary in every profession and it is equally important in the childcare sector. Childcare professionals must be on time for work every day. Parents leave children in their care and may be in a hurry to be at work. If a childcare professional says that they are going to do something, they must carry it out (e.g. planning various exercises and implementing them with the children).

Highly skilled

The childcare professional should have the necessary qualifications to work in various areas of childcare, e.g. crèche, playschool and afterschool. They must be familiar with the educational needs of children. They must have indepth knowledge in areas such as child development, Aistear and Síolta and legislation relevant to the childcare sector. They should be familiar with ILPs of children and the purpose of planning. The childcare professional should strive to be a lifelong learner and keep up to date with qualifications and continuous professional development (CPD).

Creative

Childcare professionals should be open to new ideas and challenges. They can experiment with different activities and also allow the children to be creative, which will make for an attractive classroom environment. Each child is a different type of learner: children have different ways of learning new information. It is important for all childcare professionals to be aware of the different types of learners, as explained by Howard Gardner in his multiple intelligences theory (1983). It is also important that a variety of activities are implemented to complement each learning style.

Different learning styles are detailed below.

- **Linguistic**

  Children with strengths in linguistic intelligence are particularly good with words and languages and have a good memory. They enjoy such activities as reading, listening to stories and taking about what they have learned.

- **Naturalist**

  Children with a naturalist intelligence find nature and the outdoors particularly stimulating and enjoy spending time close to nature. In order to cater for naturalist intelligence, practitioners can ensure children have opportunities to do activities outdoors, e.g. nature walks, collecting and comparing items for a nature table, planting flowers and classifying different plants and animal species.

- **Visual/Spatial**

  Children with visual/spatial intelligence are quite artistic and work well with images. They like to draw and paint. Practitioners can ensure that a wide variety of art materials are available for the children and art is done with the children on regular basis.

- **Logical/Mathematical**

  Children with logical/mathematical intelligence work well with numbers. They have strong reasoning skills and a good ability to solve problems. Suitable activities for the children include games of patterns and numbers and puzzles.

- **Bodily Kinesthetic**

  Children with this kind of intelligence have a greater ability to learn when they are involved in practical activities and doing things rather than just being told or reading about it. They tend to be good at physical activities and enjoy performing, e.g. dance, drama and sports. They are also good at making things. Practitioners can ensure they provide children with a variety of practical materials so they can work using a hands-on approach and also ensure that dance and drama are a regular part of the weekly ECEC routine.

- **Intrapersonal**

  Children with good intrapersonal intelligence tend to enjoy working and exploring independently. They are good at forming ideas and problem solving. Practitioners must ensure that children are given opportunities to work alone on activities as well as in groups.

- **Interpersonal**

  Children with interpersonal intelligence are good at considering other people and their feelings. They communicate well in a group and can learn a lot from such interaction. (This intelligence is the opposite of intrapersonal.) Practitioners should ensure to provide opportunities for children to work in groups doing different exercises and activities, e.g. two or three children working together to make a large jigsaw.

- **Musical/Rhythmic**
  Children with musical intelligence are strong singers; they have a good ability to play musical instruments and they understand rhythm and sound. They also enjoy listening to music. Practitioners can ensure that music is a regular part of the classroom routine, with action songs and nursery rhymes. ECEC settings often have a Gymboree class weekly or fortnightly that the children can enjoy.

Trustworthy
The childcare professional must be trustworthy. They care for parents' most valuable asset: children. They will often know very personal information regarding children. This information should be kept strictly confidential, except in the case where a childcare professional is concerned for the welfare and safety of the child.

Levelheaded
A childcare professional must be ready to deal with the unexpected when working in an environment with children. Emergencies can occur at any time and they must be dealt with in a calm and efficient manner.

Passionate
The childcare professional should be passionate about their chosen career. They should show interest and enthusiasm on a daily basis. They should show a genuine love for their job and really believe that what they do is of benefit to the children. They should not be working with children if this is a job they are doing for the sake of having a job. A lack of passion can lead to frustration and can have negative effects on the professional and also the children, since children can pick up on this energy very quickly.

Understanding
The childcare professional must be an understanding person. They should be aware of the difficulties they are liable to come upon and the possible difficulties that children may come across as they are learning new information and skills. Practitioners must be sympathetic and offer support to parents if necessary.

Observant
The childcare professional is required to be an acute observer. They must observe the children in their care on a regular basis and keep records of these observations. Observations can be

very useful. They can show how a child is progressing developmentally or establish if any changes need to be made to the environment. For instance, the childcare professional could see from an observation that a child needs extra guidance with an activity. Childcare professionals can observe children individually and in groups, using techniques such as narrative, checklists, time sampling, etc..

Self-aware

Childcare professionals must be self-aware. Self-awareness is how we manage ourselves and our behaviour and how we mix with other people. This is relevant, especially when working as part of the childcare team. Through being self-aware, professionals have the ability to make good choices, be motivated and work towards reaching goals.

Energetic

Children will respond positively to childcare professionals who are energetic and enthusiastic. Children can absorb this energy and it can lead to a very positive early childhood environment.

Values of a Childcare Professional

A value can be defined as a belief, set of beliefs or philosophy that is particularly meaningful for a person. Values are the issues people feel strongly about. If a person has values, this shows that they have good intentions; this can also be known as a code of ethics. Ethics are similar to a set of rules that are usually strictly enforced by supervisors and managers. A set of core values or ethics is essential when working in the childcare sector, since this ensures that professionals have priorities and can distinguish what is acceptable and unacceptable professional behaviour. Values will also help to ensure good practice. Whether we are consciously aware of them or not, every individual has a core set of personal values. Values can be quite simple and straightforward, e.g. a belief in punctuality or organisation. Having a clear set of values allows a person to become aware of what is important in life. Whatever a person's values may be, if values are truly believed and implemented they can make a significant impact on our lives. Childcare professionals in particular may possess some of the values that follow.

Welfare of the Children

Childcare professionals value the welfare of the children in their care. They have a very important job to do and are entrusted with children of a very vulnerable age. The childcare professional will value the opinions of children and ensure they have expectations of children according to their age and stage of development. The childcare professional will value the use of appropriate behaviour management techniques, e.g. speaking to the child at their level or using positive discipline (where the child is redirected to another activity, rather than any kind of threats, punishments or humiliation).

Suitable and Safe Environment

Childcare professionals value keeping children safe and preventing them from accidents or any kind of harm. They will be responsible and ensure that they adhere to the policies and procedures of the education setting, particularly in the event of an emergency occurring. The childcare professional will ensure that they implement appropriate lessons and activities using a range of suitable materials. Activities should be planned well and should build on children's achievements and interests. The children's learning and development will be the main priority of the professional.

Working in Partnership with Parents

Childcare professionals value the fact that parents are the children's main caregivers; childcare professionals should consult and share information with parents on a daily basis. Childcare professionals can welcome parents to their ECEC setting and answer any questions or queries they may have. They have respect for parents at all times.

The Value of Play

Play is a very valuable method of helping children to learn. Play helps to foster independence and creativity. Children should be allowed to initiate their own play and be given regular encouragement by the professional. Childcare professionals can provide opportunities for structured play, free play, pretend play, and so on.

Love of the Job

If a person does not enjoy their job it is impossible for them to hide it. Children can pick up on this; therefore, it is vital that the childcare practitioner gets fulfilment from their job. They must be the best that they can possible be in order to face up to the everyday challenges of the job. They must be motivated. A job with children is not something that you take on unless you plan on being dedicated. Working with children can be very rewarding, however.

Professional Development

Childcare workers may value continuing professional development (CPD) and the need to keep up to date with developments with the childcare area. Childcare professionals should have achieved at least entry level qualifications (QQI Level 5 or equivalent) and supervisors and managers should have further qualifications (QQI Level 6 or equivalent).

Equality of Opportunity

The childcare professional values that all children are treated equally in the ECEC setting and that they are provided with equal opportunities and freedom of choice as to what activities and exercises they would like to complete. All children are able to participate in all exercises.

By childcare professionals investing in CPD they are reassured that they have access to new information and materials relating to the childcare sector and are doing their best to provide the best quality ECEC to children.

'The Model Framework for Education, Training and Professional Development in the Early Childhood Care and Education Sector' explains in detail the requirements for professional development throughout childcare education and training. Childcare professionals can ensure knowledge in child development, hygiene, nutrition and safety, among other things. The model framework allows people that are working in the childcare sector to establish where they are in relation to their own learning and professional development: examining their role in the childcare sector, assessing the professional development they have completed and deciding what they would like to learn in the future. The model framework explains the fact that there are many different routes available regarding professional development. People can learn through experience and also through education and training.

Methods of CPD

Within the childcare sector there is a wide range of courses suitable to all learners' needs. Therefore, it is very important that each course is considered and researched well. Practitioners should ensure that a chosen course is the best one for them and that it satisfies the qualifications needed. Checking courses carefully ensures there is no inconvenience of realising that it is not suitable. The City/County Childcare Committees (CCCs) and National Voluntary Childcare Organisations will be able to support practitioners who wish to find out more about CPD.

Some examples of professional development are listed below.

- Professionals may attend meetings and conferences with other similar professionals, or colleagues in other settings. These meetings may be of short duration. Here they can discuss best practice and speak about their experiences.
- Every ECEC setting should partake in regular staff meetings to discuss problems or concerns staff may have, allowing them to work together on certain ideas or issues. This can also be a good time for staff to help each other with tasks and to receive constructive criticism feedback.
- E-Learning: A simple yet effective method of learning comes from having internet access, where professionals can use online resources. An activity like this one allows learners to access more information on particular subjects.
- Short courses and workshops are useful forms of professional development. Some may be short in duration and this is good if there is only one particular area to be studied, e.g. first aid, manual handling, food hygiene. It would be common practice for professionals to attend such courses over one or two days and receive a 'record of attendance' certificate at the end.

- Professionals can increase their learning by completing observations of other professionals within the sector. This technique is also very useful for students that are unqualified: they can observe best practice from qualified and experienced staff.
- Professional learning can come from engaging in reflective practice. Staff should keep a journal or diary for their own personal reflections. This can be a good source of learning. They can write down their thoughts, strengths and weakness, along with the ways in which they can improve their performance. Professionals can then look back over previous reflections from time to time to see how their personal and professional learning has developed.
- Full- and part-time courses: FÁS has played an important role in widening access to education and training courses for childcare practitioners regarding the Community Employment (CE) scheme, which facilitates long-term unemployed people to re-enter the workforce by providing them with a 'return to work routine'. Local further education colleges (e.g. VECs) have a wide range of available childcare courses and provide regular informative brochures explaining the length of the course, the price, the modules covered and the employment opportunities after completion of the course.

Employers can be a good source of support. Professionals may decide that a full-time course is the right option for them and will take a career break, particularly if completing a university course. They may even decide to complete such a course at night.

Employers from time to time may pay for staff to complete courses, particularly short courses. While employers initially have to bear the expense, they will also benefit by their staff being better qualified. Many institutions can offer a discount rate for people claiming social welfare; this is done to ensure that courses are accessible to everyone.

The Further Education and Training Awards Council (FETAC) was the statutory awarding body for further education and training in Ireland, which has now amalgamated with HETAC, NQA and IUQB to form QQI. QQI will continue to provide quality-assured awards as part of the National Framework of Qualifications (NFQ). FETAC determines the required standards and award requirements, validates programmes leading to the awards and carefully programmes and services to ensure quality assurance (www.fetac.ie/fetac/aboutfetac.htm).

The National Framework of Qualifications (NFQ) allows learners to compare their qualifications and to ensure that they are quality assured and recognised at home and abroad (www.nfq.ie/nfq/en/).

Learners that complete part-time and full-time courses in particular will most likely be required to complete written assignments. They will be given assignment briefs devised by the course tutor as well as appropriate guidelines on completing the assignment and a marking scheme so learners can see where marks are earned. In order to be certified, learners need a minimum percentage to pass (e.g. 50 per cent). Their work will be corrected by the tutor. The marks are then verified with an external assessor marker from QQI. This ensures best practice. Learners may be required to complete essays over a number of weeks or complete exams that include long and short questions. Learners are likely to spend some time at work placement, if not already working in the area. Here they may need to complete a reflective diary showing how the time was spent on placement, the activities/lessons completed and details of interactions with other staff members. The National Framework of Qualifications (NFQ) will be developed further by QQI, resulting in ever greater opportunities for students.

The Value of Good Interpersonal Skills

Interpersonal skills are how people relate to each other. We use interpersonal skills every day to communicate and interact with other people, individually and in groups. Interpersonal skills include confidence, the ability to listen and understand, problem-solving skills, decision-making skills and the ability to manage personal stress. Interpersonal skills are particularly important when working with children. Practitioners must communicate with them and form positive relationships with them and their parents. Practitioners can use interpersonal skills to manage situations and conflicts that may arise.

Practitioners are required to be role models for children, which includes helping them to develop good interpersonal skills themselves. Interpersonal skills are also important because the childcare professional will most likely be working as part of a term. Interpersonal skills are also sometimes referred to as social skills, people skills, soft skills or life skills.

Respect

The importance of respect was mentioned earlier in the chapter. It is a vital skill but it is also one that people can find difficult to show, particularly if there is (or has been) conflict between people. Childcare professionals should ensure that they do their very best to be respectful to every person, even those with different opinions from their own. Practitioners must be respectful of parents, colleagues and children.

Empathy

Practitioners should try to understand the other person's point of view. Empathy is the reason we feel bad when someone has bad luck. Empathy is an essential interpersonal skill that is best fostered in people at an early age.

Communication

Good communication skills are vital when working with children. Childcare professionals must ensure they have good listening skills: children like to feel that they are being listened to. Childcare professionals should practise attentive listening, not merely listening while doing something or talking to someone. Communication also involves those things that are not said, i.e. non verbal communication (body language, expressions and posture). Professionals will know the children in their care. They will recognise a child's facial expressions and how they usually act during the day. Quite often practitioners are among the first to know if there is something wrong with a particular child. Good speaking skills are necessary when in conversation with parents also.

- **Assertiveness**
  Childcare professionals must be able to listen to other people and their points of view, without always thinking that they themselves are in the right. Good practitioners are able to give their opinions firmly and assertively, without seeming harsh or angry.
- **Humour**
  Having a sense of humour is an important quality when working with children. Enjoying their company and helping them to learn through play will be much easier with a sense of humour.
- **Reflection**
  Reflection on one's own practice is an important role for all childcare professionals. This is the ability to consider strengths, weakness and areas that could be improved. Practitioners are required to put the children's needs before their own.
- **Conflict avoidance**
  Being able to avoid conflict or arguments is an important aspect. Conflict avoidance is about preventing conflict from happening in the first place. To effectively avoid conflict, people should be honest and genuine while being respectful to other people.

Section 2: Communication
Guidelines for Good Communication

The following are some guidelines for effective communication in the ECEC setting.

1   When practitioners speak in a room of ten children, a child may not understand who exactly is being spoken to. If this is the case, practitioners should go over to the child and call their name in a friendly manner to ensure their full attention. Avoid calling them across the room or speaking to them if they are surrounded by noise: the child may not understand what is being said. Also, give the child time to speak: they may need to think for a few seconds if they are asked a question.

2   Keep sentences short and to the point. If you are asking a child to do something, don't ask them to do several things at once; this complicates things. Repeat what is required from the children a number of times to ensure they have understood.

3   Communication is a very basic requirement when working with children. It is important that childcare workers communicate well with children so that children know and understand what is expected of them and so that they can learn good communication skills at an early age. Quite often, childcare workers may unintentionally send mixed messages to children and children lack clarity on what is being asked of them.

4   Ensure that you speak to children at their level, especially when speaking with children on a one-one basis. It may be necessary to bend down to do this; this will allow eye contact and will allow the child to see that they have your undivided attention.

5   Always use correct grammar and pronunciation when speaking to children and speak slowly and clearly.

6   Avoid sarcasm: children do not understand sarcasm and it is not a very professional manner in which to act.

7   Explain to the children what you are doing and why: it helps them to know what is happening.

Types of Communication

Verbal Communication

Speaking

The primary form of communication is by speaking to each other, which is learned automatically by most people from infancy. When people are successful in learning a language, it does not necessarily mean that they have good speaking skills. In order to have good speaking skills, people must practise speaking clearly. Practitioners must speak clearly to children at all times and ensure correct pronunciation of words.

Listening

Listening is a very important communication skill: without it, information can easily be misunderstood. Practitioners are required to be good listeners, not only for the children but for parents also. By listening carefully, it allows you to notice what is only being partially said or not being said at all.

Reading

Practitioners can communicate to children by reading them a story. Questioning is also relevant here: once the story is read, practitioners can ask the children questions about what they have just heard.

Writing

Adults can communicate by writing something for the children, e.g. letters and words. Children can communicate by writing, painting or drawing.

Asking Questions

Practitioners can communicate with children by asking for their opinions on certain things, and asking them how they feel.

Non-verbal Communication

As well as verbal communication used by childcare professionals, non-verbal communication is also commonly used. Non-verbal communication is communication without any words. It includes facial expression, body language, gesture and tone of voice.

Facial Expression

Facial expression can show what people are feeling and thinking. We can make many different facial expressions: a wink, a disapproving glance, a smile, a frown, etc. When greeting someone using non-verbal communication, a simple smile is often sufficient and will ensure that the person knows that you are happy to see them.

Sign Language

Irish Sign Language, which is used by the deaf community in Ireland, Lámh, is a manual signing system used by both children and adults with communication difficulties. There is also a communication system that uses pictures rather than words, PECS, which is particularly useful for children with autism.

Body Language

Body language can also show us how a person is feeling, e.g. if a child sits at the table with their arms folded this can suggest that they are not happy and can show they are defensive. Practitioners must interact with children and parents by standing up straight and ensuring that they make eye contact when communicating.

Gesture

Gesture is an important part of non-verbal communication. Gestures involve moving a part of the body that shows something in the message. For example, a shrug of the shoulders shows you are unsure about something and throwing your arms up in the air can show that you are angry or excited. When meeting and greeting a child or parent, practitioners may simply shake their hand.

Tone of Voice

The tone of a person's voice (its volume and pitch) can add considerable meaning to a sentence. When words are said in a hesitant tone, this may convey that a person is apprehensive or unsure. A high-pitched tone can show that a person is content or feeling positive. Practitioners should greet children and parents with a positive tone.

Imparting Information to Parents

Imparting information means providing information. Practitioners will have regular correspondence with parents in relation to many different things. There are many ways to provide parents with information, some of which are detailed below.

Parent–Teacher Meetings

This particular method is a well-known way of meeting with parents to discuss how their child is progressing academically with the work they complete, as well as socially with other children.

Newsletters

Regular newsletters or leaflets can inform parents of interesting upcoming events or events completed in the past. Practitioners often do not have time to tell all parents about all important activities completed; therefore, a newsletter is a very good idea. It can be designed simply on any computer and it can be printed out or e-mailed.

Websites

Many education facilities now have their own website where parents can be kept up to date with what is happening on a daily basis. The website can explain a particular ethos or mission statement and can be equipped with links to other interesting websites.

Notice Boards
Any important information that parents need to know urgently can be put on the notice board. While parents are waiting to collect their children, they can be encourage to have a read of the notice board.

Academic Calendar
An academic calendar can be provided to parents at the beginning of a new term. It will show essential dates to remember, e.g. holidays or periods of closure.

Notes
A very useful way to send information to individual parents can be to put a note in their child's bag.

Texts
Group texting is also a good idea. This is where the setting can send the same text to all parents. It is a quick and convenient way of sending reminders.

Imparting Information to Children

There are many ways to provide children with information, some of which are detailed below.

Puppet Shows
Puppet shows have the potential to provide great entertainment to children. Puppet shows also tell facts or a story. Children will usually be very interested and attentive and exhibit great concentration skills.

Poetry, Storytelling and Songs
Practitioners can provide children with information through a poem, story or song. Children often receive great enjoyment from such activities and will ask for the activity to be repeated.

Posters and Picture Books
Posters and picture books can provide information and can be useful in a lesson. During circle time, for example, practitioners can use posters or picture books to give more information on a topic being discussed.

Effective Interaction with Parents

Good communication with parents is just as important as communication with children. Practitioners must develop a good relationship with parents, particularly first-time parents who may require more interaction and advice. Practitioners should express empathy and should be helpful to parents if they have any concerns. Parents must be treated equally and in a friendly manner. It is also important to remember that parents are not your friends: even if you know them quite well, there must always be a professional distance.

If possible, have an open-door policy and encourage parents to call in on a regular basis. Parents can call in and sit in and observe. They can look at the materials and see the day-to day-schedule and the general classroom environment. Not every practice may have this facility. There can be a fear that having parents in the setting (especially at the beginning of a new school term in September) will unsettle the children. However, having this policy in place will allow parents to experience firsthand what happens in the setting.

Keep parents involved by asking for their opinions or help, perhaps around family cultures and values. If the parents have a qualification that would allow them to call in and talk to the children about their profession, this can be encouraged.

Provide regular correspondence. Have a chat with parents when they drop/collect their child and ensure that you use eye contact and good interpersonal skills.

Be helpful if parents have any concerns. If you don't know the answer to their questions, offer to ask a colleague or supervisor and explain that you can talk again with the parent at a later date when you have all of the information.

Confidentiality

Confidentiality is a very important topic when working with children and their parents.

Childcare workers have access to very confidential information. When a child is enrolled in a setting, parents have to include on the application form such details as address, medical history and culture. There must be a suitable and safe area to store such information. A policy can be put in place to ensure that all staff are aware of this. Practitioners must never gossip about parents or their children.

Staff must be aware that revealing information on children or their families is prohibited unless distinct permission has been granted by parents. The Child Care (Pre-School) Regulations 2006 state clearly that information on children in ECEC settings is permitted by inspection only to parents of a child attending the service (but only regarding information entered in the register concerning their *own* child) or to a person working in the pre-school service who is authorised by the person carrying out the service and one other authorised person.

Practitioners do, however, have a duty to share information if they suspect incidents of child abuse. Some other information is required to be shared, e.g. information on allergies and a list of the people nominated to collect the child.

Section 3: Teamwork

Teams

When you are working with children it is important to remember that it is unlikely you will be working alone. Unless you are working as a sole childminder, you are likely to be working alongside others. In the majority of ECEC settings there are managers and team leaders, but there are also many teams. Teams are groups of people in any number (small or large) who work together to achieve a particular goal. Everyone is on the same side. This is always a very valuable concept to remember when working as a team: each member is working on the same task or goal, even if there are differences of opinion.

It is very common for childcare professionals to work as part of a team that is multi-disciplinary, i.e. there are a number of different professions as part of the same team (e.g. manager, team leader, Montessori teacher, etc.). All team members must work together in a team to ensure that they meet all of the children's individual needs. This task is too big for one individual member to complete, so it requires people to work together to ensure that this happens.

Children rely on practitioners to do their very best to provide for them. The main goal that childcare professionals will be working for is an effective education setting for children and the implementation of an appropriate curriculum. Teamwork is about using your skills and qualities effectively so that they can complement those of other people in the team. Effective teamwork helps the education setting to run efficiently. It is important that there is a sense of community in every team, so that everyone can establish good working relationships.

Working as part of a team requires a person to have many qualities, e.g. patience, respect and motivation. Teams are comprised of different people with different strengths and weakness and different values and opinions. People will work differently. This is what can make a team succeed: different people coming together, sharing ideas and formulating new ones. It is also how co-workers can establish very positive work relationships.

Why Do ECEC Practitioners Work in Teams?

There are many reasons why childcare practitioners work in teams in an ECEC setting, some of which are listed below.

1   Teamwork allows for effective brainstorming, ensuring that valuable ideas can be developed and shared among the team.
2   Staff that work in teams can be good role models for children. Parents too can see that teamwork is a valuable part of the ECEC setting, which shows that team members are interested, motivated and ensuring best practice.

- Was the activity the right length of time?
- Would you need more time to do a similar activity in the future?
- Would you need less time to do a similar activity in the future?

Action Plan

Drawing on the conclusions you have made, you can make a plan of action for the future. Ask yourself the following questions:

- What changes would you make for the future?
- What is your professional learning?
- How have you become a better practitioner as a result of completing this exercise?

Peer Evaluation

Peer review is a process used for checking or evaluating the work or performance of colleagues of or people in a similar area. This is to ensure consistency with specific criteria. Peer review is used in teams so that errors can be identified quite quickly. Quite often it is easier for *other* people to notice mistakes and find errors in work or performance; they will be able to make a more impartial evaluation of things. Peer evaluation ensures the highest standards of performance.

Early Care and Education Practice (5N1770): Assessment Guidelines

Note: This chapter provides suggested guidelines for the assessment of module 5N1770, awarded by QQI. While students will find these guidelines helpful, they should follow closely the brief and instructions given by their own particular college in all instances.

Marks are awarded under the following headings:

- Assignment 1: Implementation of one care and one educational routine in an ECEC setting (30%)
- Assignment 2: Guide to the ECEC sector in Ireland (30%)
- Learner Record: Ten reflective diary entries (40%)

Assignment 1

For this assignment, you are required to plan, implement and evaluate **one** care and **one** education routine in the ECEC setting.

Sample Brief

Early Care and Education Practice (5N1770): Assignment Brief (30%)
Assignment 1: Implementation of *one* care and *one* educational routine in an ECEC setting.
For this assignment, you are required to plan, implement and evaluate **one** care and **one** education routine in the ECEC setting.

1   Title page
2   Table of contents

For each routine:

3   Introduction: aim, objectives and rationale
4   Details of planning and implementation of the chosen routine
5   Appropriate references to legislation, policies and principles of good practice
6   Show how the routine supports equality and diversity
7   Evaluate the routine in terms of its effectiveness and your role in completing the routine
8   Personal learning gained
9   Recommendations on how the routine could be improved upon

For the overall assignment:

10   References
11   Appendices

Guidelines

Title Page

The title page will normally show your name and PPS number. It will give details of the module title and the title of your assignment, e.g. Early Care and Education Practice (5N1770): Assignment 1 – Care and Education Routines.

Table of Contents

Provide a list of contents with page numbers. This will be done at the very end, when you know exactly what is in your assignment and on which page each section appears.

For each routine:

Introduction: Aim, Objectives and Rationale

You must state your general aim, i.e. what it is you are hoping to achieve in your assignment. Your aim could be: 'To choose, plan, implement and evaluate a suitable care/education routine making reference to relevant legislation, policies and principles of good practice'.

Break down the aim of your assignment into smaller parts or objectives. Your objectives could be to:

- Investigate the various care routines currently being practised in the setting and choose one that I feel is important and that I could learn from
- Investigate any legislation, policies or principles of good practice relevant to my chosen routine
- Plan and implement my routine in an organised and systematic way
- Explain how my routine supports equality and diversity.

You must provide a rationale. Explain your reasons for choosing the particular routine. Two or three reasons usually suffice. For example: 'I chose sleep as my care routine. I feel that this is one of the most important routines in ECEC settings because of its significant health and safety implications.'

Details of Planning and Implementation of the Chosen Routine

Give a detailed description of how you researched, planned and carried out the chosen routine. Include details of discussions with supervisors and documentation you read in preparation for carrying out the routine. Detail any theory you read in preparation for carrying out the routine. For example, if sleep was one of your chosen routines, you can explain how you downloaded the Sudden Infant Death Association's leaflet on safe sleep and you read the research articles on their website. Ensure that you provide relevant details. Write down any equipment, materials or resources you collected while planning the routine. Give a step-by-step guide to how you carried out the routine.

Appropriate References to Legislation, Policies and Principles of Good Practice

- **Legislation (Safety, Health and Welfare at Work Act 2005)**

  Here you detail any pieces of legislation you think are related to your chosen routine. For example, if you chose nappy changing as your care routine, the Safety, Health and Welfare at Work Act 2005 could be applicable.

  If there were any children with special needs in the group for your education routine, you could write about the Education of Persons with Special Educational Needs Act 2004.

■ **Policies**

Here you should detail any policies the setting has in place in relation to the routine you have chosen. For example, if you chose nappy changing you could include details of the setting's policy and routine for this aspect of care, together with a copy of their nappy changing log forms.

■ **Principles of good practice**

Here you refer to relevant parts of (1) the Child Care (Pre-School) Regulations 2006, (2) the National Standards for Pre-School Services 2010, (3) Department of Health and Children: Food and Nutrition Guidelines for Pre-School Services (if your chosen routine was a feeding routine) and (4) Síolta and Aistear (which are particularly relevant for education routines)

Show How the Routine Supports Equality and Diversity

Chapter 3 of this book will give you some ideas as to how equality and diversity relate to education and care routines.

Care routines

■ Sleep routine: Are the sleeping facilities in the setting such that a worker with a physical disability could utilise them?

■ Toileting routines: Are the toileting facilities suitable for children who are wheelchair users?

■ Nappy changing routines: Could a worker with a disability change a baby safely using current nappy changing facilities or are all changing tables too high?

■ Feeding routines: Are children's food needs and preferences catered for, e.g. vegetarian? Is there adapted feeding equipment available for children with special needs to improve grip and strength and prevent bowls slipping and food spillages?

■ Hand washing routines: Have you checked for allergies? Are all soap products hypoallergenic? Are there any children with additional requirements, e.g. children with eczema who may need to have an emollient cream applied after hand washing?

Education routines

■ Story telling routines: Can all children see the book and your face while storytelling? How do you ensure this? Do you choose books that depict different ethnic grouping, family structures, gender roles, abilities and disabilities and ages in a positive light?

■ Circle time routines: Are all children given an equal opportunity to participate in circle time? How do you ensure this? Do you discuss topics related to equality and diversity?

Evaluate the Routine in Terms of its Effectiveness and Your Role in Completing the Routine

In this section, state very clearly what you felt was effective (good) or ineffective (not so good) about your routine. You should consider your planning and the sequence of your implementation. You should consider the routine itself: are there improvements that could be made? Routines, even if they are long established, can always be improved upon.

With education routines, you should consider your planning and implementation plus whether the routine was age- and stage-appropriate and what the children gained from it. Likewise, you need to state very clearly what you felt was not so effective. For example: 'I felt that the story I chose as part of my storytelling routine was too long and the plot too complex. Children began to lose interest towards the second half of the session. I decided to finish the story quickly rather than persevere and I will choose a more age- and stage-appropriate book the next time.'

You should also consider things like the timing of the routine; story time normally occurs directly after lunch. For example: 'I felt that the timing of this was good in that children were relaxed and they enjoyed sitting down for a period of time after lunch.'

Personal Learning Gained

Record in a very specific way what you learned from carrying out your routine. Good marks will not be awarded for very vague statements, so be specific.

For example: 'I now understand how to position a baby in the safe sleep position:

- Babies should be put to sleep on their backs. Older babies and children may change position themselves during sleep, but should be put down on their backs.
- Feet to foot – babies' feet should be at the bottom of the cot.
- Use sheets and aerated blankets, not fluffy or bulky duvets. Tuck sheets and blankets securely, but not tightly. Use a firm, clean, well-fitting mattress.
- Make sure babies' heads remain uncovered during sleep.
- There should be no pillows, toys, cot bumpers or other items in the cot with a baby.'

Recommendations on How the Routine Could Be Improved Upon

Most routines are very well thought out in settings, so this section may be challenging for you to write about. You have to come up with ideas as to how the routine you have chosen could be improved upon. For example:

'As part of their feeding routine, children are given a set period of time to eat their dinner. I feel that some children require more time than others and that, therefore, dinner time should be more flexible. If some children require more time to finish than others, they should be permitted that time. Also, I feel that mealtimes should be social times – I feel that staff should eat with children where possible.'

References
Correctly list all sources of information used in the assignment e.g. books, internet articles, etc. (See Appendix 7, p. 200, for guidance.)

Appendices
Supply any additional information that is relevant to your work.

Assignment 2

For this assignment, you are required to investigate and present an assignment detailing a number of different aspects of the ECEC sector in Ireland.

Sample Brief

Early Care and Education Practice (5N1770): Assignment Brief (30%)
Assignment 2: A Guide to the ECEC sector in Ireland.
For this assignment, you are required to investigate and detail a number of different aspects of the ECEC sector in Ireland. Please present your findings under the following headings:

1   Title page
2   Table of contents
3   Introduction: aim, objectives and rationale
4   Provide a comprehensive profile of the history of the ECEC sector in Ireland
5   Explain the rights of the child in the context of the ECEC setting
6   Describe the ECEC sector and its range of occupations
7   Detail the qualifications and experience needed for work associated with one occupation in the ECEC sector
8   Examine and discuss the employment and career opportunities in the ECEC sector
9   References
10   Appendices

Guidelines
Title Page
The title page will normally show your name and PPS number. It will give details of the module title and the title of your assignment, e.g. Early Care and Education Practice (5N1770): Assignment 2 – A Guide to the ECEC sector in Ireland.

Table of Contents

Provide a list of contents with page numbers. This will be done at the very end, when you know exactly what is in your assignment and on which page each section appears.

Introduction: Aim, Objectives and Rationale

You must state your general aim, i.e. what it is you are hoping to achieve in your assignment. Your aim could be: 'To present an informative and comprehensive overview of the childcare sector in Ireland today'.

Break down the aim of your assignment into smaller parts or objectives. Your objectives could be to:

- Trace and present the history of ECEC provision in Ireland
- Explain the rights of the child in the context of an ECEC setting
- Describe the ECEC sector and its range of occupations
- Detail the qualifications and experience needed for work associated with one occupation in the ECEC sector
- Examine and discuss the employment and career opportunities in the childcare sector.

You must provide a rationale. Explain why you think it is important to undertake an assignment such as this. For example:

'Since this is my chosen career, it is important that I have a thorough understanding of ECEC provision in Ireland. It is important for me to see how ECEC has progressed over the years and also, from a vocational point of view, to understand what is out there for me when I qualify as an ECEC practitioner. This assignment will also help me to investigate possible progression routes in this field on completion of my current course of study.'

Provide a Comprehensive Profile of the History of the ECEC sector in Ireland

Give a comprehensive account of the history of ECEC provision in Ireland. Chapter 1 will provide you with information for this part of your assignment. Do not copy information directly from this source (or any other). Read widely and put information into your own words. If you do take information directly, reference it accordingly.

Explain the Rights of the Child in the Context of an ECEC Setting

Chapter 2 of this book deals extensively with this aspect of ECEC provision. You should consider how all aspects of legislation, policies, practices and procedures discussed in this chapter promote the rights of the child.

Describe the ECEC Sector and its Range of Occupations

Describe the ECEC sector in terms of *all* of its occupations. You should take a broad approach to this and consider *everyone* involved in ECEC provision:

- HSE personnel: inspectors, social workers, family support workers, psychologists, therapists, public health nurses, etc.
- City/County Childcare Committees
- Managers of settings/childcare practitioners
- Special needs assistants
- Primary school teachers.

Chapter 1 of this book will assist you with this section.

Detail the Qualifications and Experience Needed for Work Associated with One Occupation in the ECEC Sector

Choose *one* of the occupations mentioned above. Research this occupation in detail and present your findings.

Examine and Discuss the Employment and Career Opportunities in the Childcare Sector

This section of your assignment asks you to investigate what opportunities are available to you after you have completed your course. Opportunities can be categorised under the following two headings.

- Join the workforce

  Research and present information on what jobs are available at present in your region. Detail the qualifications and experience required and the pay and conditions on offer. You may like to include actual job advertisements in your appendix.
- Undertake further training

  Research and present information on the training opportunities available to you in the future. Describe where these opportunities will lead. It could be worth investigating what opportunities further qualifications and training would lead to in countries where ECEC services are more graduate led (e.g. Australia and New Zealand).

Learner Record

For this assignment you are required to present *ten* complete diary entries to include ten reflections based on your experiences while on work placement.

Sample Brief

Early Care and Education Practice (5N1770): Learner Record (40%)
Learner Record: Ten Reflective Diaries.
For this assignment you are required to present *ten* complete diary entries to include ten
reflections based on your experiences while on work placement.

1   Title page
2   Table of contents
3   Details of setting

For each diary:

4   Diary entry
5   Reflection on diary entry

For the overall assignment:

6   Evaluation

Guidelines

Title Page

The title page will normally show your name and PPS number. It will give details of the
module title and the title of your assignment, e.g. Early Care and Education Practice
(5N1770): Learner Record.

Table of Contents

Provide a list of contents with page numbers. This will be done at the very end, when you
know exactly what is in your assignment and on which page each section appears.

Details of Setting

The purpose of this section is to give the reader a general idea of the setting in which you are
working. You should include details of the following.

- Type of setting: full-time day care, sessional service, etc.
- Physical description of setting
- Number of children catered for: details of grouping structures, etc.
- Details of staffing in the setting
- Details of your work routine in the setting: Are you based in one room or moved around
  according to requirements?
- Overall daily routine in the setting.

For each diary entry:

Diary Entry

Provide a detailed account of your day. Include details of any observations, routines or activities you carried out with the children.

Reflection on Diary Entry

This section carries more marks than other sections because you are required to critically analyse and reflect on your experiences during the day. Each day you need to consider what you learned about each of the following elements.

■ **Practical and organisational skills**

These are the concrete skills that are part of being an effective ECEC practitioner. Ask yourself the following questions:

- Were you on time this morning?
- How did you present yourself?
- Were you dressed appropriately?
- Did you have your hair tied back?
- Were your nails free from nail polish?
- Did you wear minimal makeup or other cosmetics?
- What practical and/or organisational skills did you demonstrate today?
  For example: 'I changed a baby's nappy for the first time in the setting today. I spoke to the room leader about the routine beforehand and made sure that I had everything organised and prepared before I began.'

■ **Interpersonal skills, including effective teamwork**

Highlight incidents where you demonstrated good interpersonal and effective team working skills. Also record incidents where you felt you could improve. Ask yourself the following questions:

- How did you greet the children this morning?
- How did you greet colleagues this morning?
- Did you have any interactions with parents?
- How did you greet and relate to them?
- Did you discover anything about how the setting effectively communicates with parents?
- How did you show the children you were actively listening to them?
- Did you allow the children time to speak?
- How did you support their speech?
- Were there any incidents today where you had to comfort a child? How did you do this?

- In what ways were you encouraging and positive towards the children in your care? Give examples.
- Did you feel you were part of a team today? Explain your answer.
- Did you witness any examples of good teamwork today, e.g. sharing of knowledge? Explain your answer.
- How do staff members in the setting respect confidentiality? Did you witness any examples of this today?

■ **Willingness to learn new skills**

Describe examples where you felt you were adequately trained to carry out the task at hand. Ask yourself the following question:

- Were there any situations that occurred today where you feel you would like to receive further instruction, practice or training?

■ **Awareness and active promotion of equality and diversity**

Describe any ways in which equality and diversity was promoted today. For example: 'At story time, we read *Two Homes* by Claire Masurel. This story is about a young girl whose parents have recently divorced.'

Examples need not be as explicit as this: equality and diversity can be promoted in small ways every day, e.g. seating a very small child beside you during a storytelling activity so that they can see properly.

■ **Challenges**

Describe any challenges you faced throughout the day and explain and reflect on how you dealt with them. This is a very important part of the reflective process. You are a student, so you need not have dealt with everything perfectly! You will be awarded marks for making 'mistakes', provided you reflect on them and explain how you plan to do things better next time.

Evaluation

When you have completed all ten diary entries and reflections, you need to compile an overall evaluation of the learning record. This overall evaluation will have three sections.

■ Based on what you learned during the course of the ten entries, describe the qualities required to be an effective ECEC practitioner.

■ Choose the qualities you feel you possess. Reflect on, describe and explain how you demonstrate these qualities.

■ Choose the qualities you feel you need to work on. Reflect on, describe and explain how you will improve on these qualities.

Appendix 1: Signs and symptoms of child abuse

1. Signs and symptoms of neglect

Child neglect is the most common category of abuse. A distinction can be made between 'wilful' neglect and 'circumstantial' neglect. 'Wilful' neglect would generally incorporate a direct and deliberate deprivation by a parent/carer of a child's most basic needs, e.g. withdrawal of food, shelter, warmth, clothing, contact with others. 'Circumstantial' neglect more often may be due to stress/inability to cope by parents or carers.

Neglect is closely correlated with low socio-economic factors and corresponding physical deprivations. It is also related to parental incapacity due to learning disability, addictions or psychological disturbance.

The neglect of children is 'usually a passive form of abuse involving omission rather than acts of commission' (Skuse and Bentovim, 1994). It comprises 'both a lack of physical caretaking and supervision and a failure to fulfil the developmental needs of the child in terms of cognitive stimulation'.

Child neglect should be suspected in cases of:
- abandonment or desertion;
- children persistently being left alone without adequate care and supervision;
- malnourishment, lacking food, inappropriate food or erratic feeding;
- lack of warmth;
- lack of adequate clothing;
- inattention to basic hygiene;
- lack of protection and exposure to danger, including moral danger or lack of supervision appropriate to the child's age;
- persistent failure to attend school;
- non-organic failure to thrive, i.e. child not gaining weight due not only to malnutrition but also to emotional deprivation;
- failure to provide adequate care for the child's medical and developmental problems;
- exploited, overworked.

2. Characteristics of neglect

Child neglect is the most frequent category of abuse, both in Ireland and internationally. In addition to being the most frequently reported type of abuse; neglect is also recognised as being the most harmful. Not only does neglect generally last throughout a childhood, it also has long-term consequences into adult life. Children are more likely to die from chronic neglect than from one instance of physical abuse. It is well established that severe neglect in infancy has a serious negative impact on brain development.

Neglect is associated with, but not necessarily caused by, poverty. It is strongly correlated with parental substance misuse, domestic violence and parental mental illness and disability.

Neglect may be categorised into different types (adapted from Dubowitz, 1999):
- **Disorganised/chaotic neglect:** This is typically where parenting is inconsistent and is often found in disorganised and crises-prone families. The quality of parenting is inconsistent, with a lack of certainty and routine, often resulting in emergencies regarding accommodation, finances and food. This type of neglect results in attachment disorders, promotes anxiety in children and leads to disruptive and attention-seeking behaviour, with older children proving more difficult to control and discipline. The home may be unsafe from accidental harm, with a high incident of accidents occurring.
- **Depressed or passive neglect:** This type of neglect fits the common stereotype and is often characterised by bleak and bare accommodation, without material comfort, and with poor hygiene and little if any social and psychological stimulation. The household will have few toys and those that are there may be broken, dirty or inappropriate for age. Young children will spend long periods in cots, playpens or pushchairs. There is often a lack of food, inadequate bedding and no clean clothes. There can be a sense of hopelessness, coupled with ambivalence about improving the household situation. In such environments, children frequently are absent from school and have poor homework routines. Children subject to these circumstances are at risk of major developmental delay.
- **Chronic deprivation:** This is most likely to occur where there is the absence of a key attachment figure. It is most often found in large institutions where infants and children may be physically well cared for, but where there is no opportunity to form an attachment with an individual carer. In these situations, children are dealt with by a range of adults and their needs are seen as part of the demands of a group of children. This form of deprivation will also be associated with poor stimulation and can result in serious developmental delays.

The following points illustrate the consequences of different types of neglect for children:
- inadequate food – failure to develop;
- household hazards – accidents;
- lack of hygiene – health and social problems;
- lack of attention to health – disease;
- inadequate mental health care – suicide or delinquency;
- inadequate emotional care – behaviour and educational;
- inadequate supervision – risk-taking behaviour;
- unstable relationship – attachment problems;
- unstable living conditions – behaviour and anxiety, risk of accidents;
- exposure to domestic violence – behaviour, physical and mental health;
- community violence – anti social behaviour.

3.   Signs and symptoms of emotional neglect and abuse

Emotional neglect and abuse is found typically in a home lacking in emotional warmth. It is not necessarily associated with physical deprivation. The emotional needs of the children are not met; the parent's relationship to the child may be without empathy and devoid of emotional responsiveness.

Emotional neglect and abuse occurs when adults responsible for taking care of children are unaware of and unable (for a range of reasons) to meet their children's emotional and developmental needs. Emotional neglect and abuse is not easy to recognise because the effects are not easily observable. Skuse (1989) states that 'emotional abuse refers to the habitual verbal harassment of a child by disparagement, criticism, threat and ridicule, and the inversion of love, whereby verbal and non-verbal means of rejection and withdrawal are substituted'.

Emotional neglect and abuse can be identified with reference to the indices listed below. However, it should be noted that no one indicator is conclusive of emotional abuse. In the case of emotional abuse and neglect, it is more likely to impact negatively on a child where there is a cluster of indices, where these are persistent over time and where there is a lack of other protective factors.
- rejection;
- lack of comfort and love;
- lack of attachment;
- lack of proper stimulation (e.g. fun and play);
- lack of continuity of care (e.g. frequent moves, particularly unplanned);
- continuous lack of praise and encouragement;
- serious over-protectiveness;
- inappropriate non-physical punishment (e.g. locking in bedrooms);
- family conflicts and/or violence;
- every child who is abused sexually, physically or neglected is also emotionally abused;
- inappropriate expectations of a child relative to his/her age and stage of development.

Children who are physically and sexually abused and neglected also suffer from emotional abuse.

4.   Signs and symptoms of physical abuse

Unsatisfactory explanations, varying explanations, frequency and clustering for the following events are high indices for concern regarding physical abuse:
- bruises (see below for more detail);
- fractures;
- swollen joints;
- burns/scalds (see below for more detail);
- abrasions/lacerations;
- haemorrhages (retinal, subdural);
- damage to body organs;
- poisonings – repeated (prescribed drugs, alcohol);
- failure to thrive;
- coma/unconsciousness;
- death.

There are many different forms of physical abuse, but skin, mouth and bone injuries are the most common.

Sexual exploitation

- Involves situations of sexual victimisation where the person who is responsible for the exploitation may not have direct sexual contact with the child. Two types of this abuse are child pornography and child prostitution.
- 'Child pornography' includes still photography, videos and movies, and, more recently, computer-generated pornography.
- 'Child prostitution' for the most part involves children of latency age or in adolescence. However, children as young as 4 and 5 are known to be abused in this way.

The sexual abuses described above may be found in combination with other abuses, such as physical abuse and urination and defecation on the victim. In some cases, physical abuse is an integral part of the sexual abuse; in others, drugs and alcohol may be given to the victim.

It is important to note that physical signs may not be evident in cases of sexual abuse due to the nature of the abuse and/or the fact that the disclosure was made some time after the abuse took place.

Carers and professionals should be alert to the following physical and behavioural signs:

- bleeding from the vagina/anus;
- difficulty/pain in passing urine/faeces;
- an infection may occur secondary to sexual abuse, which may or may not be a definitive sexually transmitted disease. Professionals should be informed if a child has a persistent vaginal discharge or has warts/rash in genital area;
- noticeable and uncharacteristic change of behaviour;
- hints about sexual activity;
- age-inappropriate understanding of sexual behaviour;
- inappropriate seductive behaviour;
- sexually aggressive behaviour with others;
- uncharacteristic sexual play with peers/toys;
- unusual reluctance to join in normal activities that involve undressing, e.g. games/swimming.

Particular behavioural signs and emotional problems suggestive of child abuse in **young children (aged 0-10 years)** include:

- mood change where the child becomes withdrawn, fearful, acting out;
- lack of concentration, especially in an educational setting;
- bed wetting, soiling;
- pains, tummy aches, headaches with no evident physical cause;
- skin disorders;
- reluctance to go to bed, nightmares, changes in sleep patterns;
- school refusal;
- separation anxiety;
- loss of appetite, overeating, hiding food.

Particular behavioural signs and emotional problems suggestive of child abuse in **older children (aged 10+ years)** include:

- depression, isolation, anger;
- running away;
- drug, alcohol, solvent abuse;
- self-harm;
- suicide attempts;
- missing school or early school leaving;
- eating disorders.

All signs/indicators need careful assessment relative to the child's circumstances.

(From *Children First: National Guidance for the Protection and Welfare of Children*, pp. 70–4.)

Appendix 2: Standard Reporting Form for Reporting Child Protection and/or Welfare Concerns

FORM NUMBER: CC01:01:00

STANDARD REPORT FORM
(For reporting CP&W Concerns to the HSE)

HSE
Feidhmeannacht na Seirbhíse Sláinte
Health Service Executive

A. To Principal Social Worker/Designate: _____

1. Date of Report [   ]

2. Details of Child

Name:		Male ☐	Female ☐
Address:		DOB	Age
		School	
Alias		Correspondence address (if different)	
Telephone		Telephone	

3. Details of Persons Reporting Concern(s)

Name:		Telephone No.	
Address:		Occupation	
		Relationship to client	

Reporter wishes to remain anonymous ☐   Reporter discussed with parents/guardians ☐

4. Parents Aware of Report

	Yes	No
Are the child's parents/carers aware that this concern is being reported to the HSE?	☐	☐

5. Details of Report

(Details of concern(s), allegation(s) or incident(s) dates, times, who was present, description of any observed injuries, parent's view(s), child's view(s) if known.)

FORM NUMBER: CC01:01:00

STANDARD REPORT FORM
(For reporting CP&W Concerns to the HSE)

HSE
Feidhmeannacht na Seirbhíse Sláinte
Health Service Executive

6. Relationships

Details of Mother		Details of Father	
Name:		Name:	
Address: (if different to child)		Address: (if different to child)	
Telephone No's:		Telephone No's:	

7. Household composition

Name	Relationship	DOB	Additional Information e.g. School/ Occupation/Other:

8. Name and Address of other personnel or agencies involved with this child

	Name	Address
Social Worker		
PHN		
GP		
Hospital		
School		
Gardaí		
Pre-School/Crèche/YG		
Other (specify):		

9. Details of person(s) allegedly causing concern in relation to the child

Relationship to child:		Age		Male ☐	Female ☐
Name:			Occupation		
Address:					

10. Details of person completing form

Name:		Occupation:	
Signed		Date:	

Appendix 3: Sample Menu and Menu Template

Below is a sample five-day menu for a pre-school.

Five-day menu					
Meal	**Monday**	**Tuesday**	**Wednesday**	**Thursday**	**Friday**
Breakfast	Diluted unsweetened OJ Cornflakes with whole milk Brown/white bread toasted	Diluted unsweetened OJ Puffed rice cereal with whole milk Brown/white bread toasted	Diluted unsweetened OJ Porridge made with whole milk Brown/white bread toasted	Diluted unsweetened OJ Shredded wheat with whole milk Brown bread toasted	Diluted unsweetened OJ Wholegrain wheat cereal with whole milk Brown bread toasted
Mid-morning (10am)	Milk and crackers with cheese spread	Milk with apple slices and seedless grapes	Milk with banana	Milk with fruit yoghurt	Milk with tea brack and butter
Lunch (12 noon–1pm)	Shepherd's pie (lean mince) with peas, carrots and mashed potatoes Water to drink	Quorn lasagne with cherry tomatoes and homemade coleslaw Water to drink	Homemade beef burgers (lean mince) with tomato, lettuce and onion; oven chips Water to drink	Sweet and sour pork with rice Water to drink	Ovenbaked fish (no bones) with garden peas, carrots and mashed potatoes Water to drink
Mid-afternoon (3pm)	Yoghurt	Yoghurt	Yoghurt	Crackers with cheese spread	Yoghurt
Evening (5pm)	Toasted ham and cheese sandwich Diluted unsweetened OJ	Homemade pizza slice with tomato, olives and coleslaw Diluted unsweetened OJ	Chicken wrap with grilled chicken, tomato, lettuce and scallion (low-fat mayonnaise) Diluted unsweetened OJ	Beans on toast Diluted unsweetened OJ	Boiled eggs (mixed in a cup with a little butter) with toasted brown bread Diluted unsweetened OJ

Use the template (on the following page) to create your own sample menu.

Five-day menu

Meal	Monday	Tuesday	Wednesday	Thursday	Friday
Breakfast					
Mid-morning (10 am)					
Lunch (12 noon–1 pm)					
Mid-afternoon (3 pm)					
Evening (5 pm)					

Appendix 4: Healthy Eating Policies

- Mothers will be supported to continue breastfeeding their children.
- Infants will be held upright while bottle feeding. No bottles will be propped.
- Formula milk feeds for infants will be provided by parents and will be ready to use. Staff will not make up formula feeds.
- A weekly menu will provide the children with varied foods. This menu will be on display in advance. Recipes and food ingredients are available to parents.
- Parents are encouraged to offer menu suggestions or comments on the nutrition policy.
- All children will have suitable food available depending on their age, development and needs, using the recommended servings table as a guide.
- Breakfast will be available each morning. Parents must inform the pre-school if their child needs breakfast on arrival.
- Full-fat milk will be served with morning and afternoon snacks. A low-fat or semi-skimmed milk option will be available at parents' request for children aged 2 and upwards who eat a varied diet.
- Water will be available at all times.
- Fizzy drinks and fruit squash will not be provided.
- Diluted unsweetened fruit juice will be served with main meals.
- Children will have access to bread or fruit if they are hungry between scheduled meal and snack times.
- Children will be allowed to have dessert if they do not eat their main course.
- Parents will be advised if their child is not eating well.
- Parents of children on special diets will be asked to provide as much information as possible about suitable foods. In some cases, parents may be asked to provide food themselves.
- Carers will sit with the children when they eat and will encourage good eating habits.
- Children will sit when eating or having a drink.
- Withholding food will not be used as a form of punishment.
- Parents are asked not to send sweets, crisps and other snack foods to the pre-school.
- Birthday party food should be discussed in advance with the staff.
- All food in the pre-school will be stored, prepared and served using good food safety practices.

- Staff will receive training in relation to healthy eating and food safety.
- Children will be encouraged to play outside every day, weather permitting, to ensure they receive sunlight which helps their bodies to make vitamin D.
- This policy will be displayed in the reception area. It will be reviewed annually.

Appendix 5: Notifiable Diseases and their Causative Pathogens

Acute anterior poliomyelitis Polio virus

Ano-genital warts Human papilloma virus

Anthrax *Bacillus anthracis*

***Bacillus cereus* food-borne infection/intoxication** *Bacillus cereus*

Bacterial meningitis

Botulism *Clostridium botulinum*

Brucellosis *Brucella* spp.

***Campylobacter* infection** *Campylobacter* spp.

Carbapenem-resistant *Enterobacteriaceae* infection Carbapenem-resistant
Enterobacteriaceae

Chancroid *Haemophilus ducreyi*

Chickenpox – hospitalised cases Varicella-zoster virus

Chikungunya disease Chikungunya virus

***Chlamydia trachomatis* infection (genital)** *Chlamydia trachomatis*

Cholera *Vibrio cholerae*

***Clostridium difficile* infection** *Clostridium difficile*

***Clostridium perfringens* (type A) food-borne disease** *Clostridium perfringens*

Creutzfeldt Jakob disease

Cryptosporidiosis *Cryptosporidium parvum, hominis*

Cytomegalovirus infection (congenital) Cytomegalovirus

Dengue fever Dengue virus

Diphtheria *Corynebacterium diphtheriae or ulcerans* (toxin producing)

Echinococcosis *Echinococcus* spp.

Enterococcal bacteraemia *Enterococcus* spp. (blood)

***Escherichia coli* infection (invasive)** *Escherichia coli* (blood, CSF)

Giardiasis *Giardia lamblia*

Gonorrhoea *Neisseria gonorrhoeae*

Granuloma inguinale *Klebsiella granulomatis*

***Haemophilus influenzae* disease (invasive)** *Haemophilus influenzae*

Hepatitis A (acute) infection Hepatitis A virus

Hepatitis B (acute and chronic) infection Hepatitis B virus

Hepatitis C infection Hepatitis C virus

Herpes simplex (genital) Herpes simplex virus

Human immunodeficiency virus infection Human immunodeficiency virus

Influenza Influenza A and B virus

***Klebsiella pneumoniae* infection (invasive)** *Klebsiella pneumoniae* (blood or CSF)

Legionellosis *Legionella* spp.

Leprosy *Mycobacterium leprae*

Leptospirosis *Leptospira* spp.

Listeriosis *Listeria monocytogenes*

Lyme disease (neuroborreliosis) *Borrelia burgdorferi*

Lymphogranuloma venereum *Chlamydia trachomatis*

Malaria *Plasmodium falciparum, vivax, knowlesi, ovale, malariae*

Measles Measles virus

Meningococcal disease *Neisseria meningitidis*

Mumps Mumps virus

Non-specific urethritis

Noroviral infection Norovirus

Paratyphoid *Salmonella* Paratyphi

Pertussis *Bordetella pertussis*

Plague *Yersinia pestis*

***Pseudomonas aeruginosa* infection (invasive)** *Pseudomonas aeruginosa* (blood or CSF)

Q Fever *Coxiella burnetii*

Rabies Rabies virus

Respiratory syncytial virus infection Respiratory syncytial virus

Rotavirus infection Rotavirus

Rubella Rubella virus

Salmonellosis *Salmonella* spp. other than *S.* Typhi and *S.* Paratyphi

Severe Acute Respiratory Syndrome (SARS) SARS-associated coronavirus

Shigellosis *Shigella* spp.

Smallpox Variola virus

Staphylococcal food poisoning Enterotoxigenic *Staphylococcus aureus*

***Staphylococcus aureus* bacteraemia** *Staphylococcus aureus* (blood)

***Streptococcus* group A infection (invasive)** *Streptococcus pyogenes*

***Streptococcus* group B infection (invasive)** *Streptococcus agalactiae*

***Streptococcus pneumoniae* infection (invasive)** *Streptococcus pneumoniae*

Syphilis *Treponema pallidum*

Tetanus *Clostridium tetani*

Toxoplasmosis *Toxoplasma gondii*
Trichinosis *Trichinella* spp.
Trichomoniasis *Trichomonas vaginalis*
Tuberculosis *Mycobacterium tuberculosis* complex
Tularemia *Francisella tularensis*
Typhoid *Salmonella* Typhi
Typhus *Rickettsia prowazekii*
Verotoxigenic *Escherichia coli* infection Verotoxin producing *Escherichia coli*
Viral encephalitis
Viral haemorrhagic fevers
Viral meningitis
West Nile fever West Nile virus
Yellow fever Yellow fever virus
Yersiniosis *Yersinia enterocolitica, Yersinia pseudotuberculosis*

Appendix 6: Sample Aistear Theme

The following is an extract from *Aistear: The Early Childhood Curriculum Framework* (2009: 25–8). This section covers the theme of *Identity and Belonging* and lists its *aims*, *learning goals* and *sample learning opportunities*.

Theme: Identity and Belonging

The theme of *Identity and Belonging* is about children developing a positive sense of who they are and feeling that they are valued and respected as part of a family and community.

From birth, children develop a sense of who they are. Relationships with family members, other adults and children, friends and members of their community play a key role in building their identities. Children's sense of who they are is shaped by their characteristics, their behaviour and their understanding of themselves, their family and others. Belonging is about having a secure relationship with or a connection with a particular group of people. When children feel a sense of belonging and sense of pride in their families, their peers and their communities, they can be emotionally strong, self-assured and able to deal with challenges and difficulties. This creates an important foundation for their learning and development.

Giving children messages of respect, love, approval and encouragement enables them to develop a positive sense of who they are and a feeling that they have an important contribution to make wherever they are. Positive messages about their families, backgrounds, cultures, beliefs and languages help children to develop pride in who they are. These messages also give them confidence to voice their views and opinions, to make choices and to help shape their own learning.

By embracing difference, by exploring their own attitudes in relation to equality and diversity and by realising that their attitudes and values influence children, adults can develop the insights, self-awareness and skills that are needed to help children develop a strong sense of identity and belonging. This helps to ensure that all children are respected and valued and that they can recognise and deal with discrimination and prejudice.

Identity and belonging	
Aims	**Learning goals**
Aim 1: Children will have strong self-identities and will feel respected and affirmed as unique individuals with their own life stories.	In partnership with the adult, children will: • build respectful relationships with others • appreciate the features that make a person special and unique (name, size, hair, hand and footprint, gender, birthday) • understand that as individuals they are separate from others with their own needs, interests and abilities • have a sense of 'who they are' and be able to describe their backgrounds, strengths and abilities • feel valued and see themselves and their interests reflected in the environment • express their own ideas, preferences and needs, and have these responded to with respect and consistency.
Aim 2: Children will have a sense of group identity where links with their family and community are acknowledged and extended.	In partnership with the adult, children will: • feel that they have a place and a right to belong to the group • know that members of their family and community are positively acknowledged and welcomed • be able to share personal experiences about their own families and cultures, and come to know that there is a diversity of family structures, cultures and backgrounds • understand and take part in routines, customs, festivals and celebrations • see themselves as part of a wider community and know about their local area, including some of its places, features and people • understand the different roles of people in the community.
Aim 3: Children will be able to express their rights and show an understanding and regard for the identity, rights and views of others.	In partnership with the adult, children will: • express their views and help make decisions in matters that affect them • understand the rules and the boundaries of acceptable behaviour • interact, work co-operatively and help others • be aware of and respect others' needs, rights, feelings, culture, language, background and religious beliefs • have a sense of social justice and recognise and deal with unfair behaviour • demonstrate the skills of co-operation, responsibility, negotiation and conflict resolution.
Aim 4: Children will see themselves as capable learners.	In partnership with the adult, children will: • develop a broad range of abilities and interests • show an awareness of their own unique strengths, abilities and learning styles, and be willing to share their skills and knowledge with others • show increasing confidence and self-assurance in directing their own learning • demonstrate dispositions like curiosity, persistence and responsibility • experience learning opportunities that are based on personal interests, and linked to their home, community and culture • be motivated, and begin to think about and recognise their own progress and achievements.

Sample Learning Opportunities

Babies

The adult:

- Closely observes babies, knows their **personalities** well, respects and responds to their **individual needs and preferences** and builds on **care practices** from home:
  - knows babies' natural rhythms, supports sleeping and feeding routines and provides favourite comfort objects, e.g. blanket, teddy, soothes
  - places photographs of parents near the sleeping area and knows at least a few words in the babies' home language when that language is neither English nor Irish
  - responds appropriately to babies' feelings, e.g. soothes them when upset, builds on their curiosity, provides positive physical contact such as cuddling, hugging and holding on the lap
- Supports babies' emerging **sense of identity**:
  - helps babies understand and use their physical capabilities, e.g. encouraging them to clap hands, to reach, to smile, to wave, to point and to talk using gurgles and sounds
  - helps babies to distinguish themselves from others, e.g. says the baby's name and the names of family members, looks at and points to photographs
  - provides opportunities for babies to be with, to watch and to listen to other children
  - provides low level mirrors and reflective toys, such as activity cubes with safety mirrors attached and describes what babies see to enable them to recognise their own reflection
  - displays photos of babies and their work in the setting
  - shows the daily routine through photographs, makes portfolios of babies' constructions and paintings as they grow
  - helps babies to identify body parts by pointing to, touching, and naming them, e.g. pointing to toes, wriggling fingers, tapping heads, touching ears
- Provides opportunities for **older siblings**, **peers** and **babies** to see one another and to be together at different times during the day, optimising opportunities that will enable them to interact and communicate:
  - plans activities and events when babies, siblings, and/or older children can be together, e.g. meal times, song-time, before going home
  - ensures babies and siblings have time outside to play together regularly
- Provides babies with experiences of the **outside world**:
  - brings babies outside to explore and observe on a regular basis
  - gives babies opportunities to see the outdoors, e.g. positions babies near low level windows where they have a view outside when they are inside

- provides babies with natural items, pictures and books about nature, e.g. the weather, animals and things that happen outside such as farming, travel, or buildings
- plans visits to places in the local community such as a park, a library, a playground, a market
- brings babies to the local parent-and-baby or parent-and-toddler group.

Appendix 7: Additional Sleeping and Resting Criteria for Overnight Services

Overnight Pre-school Services

Under Regulation 4 of the Child Care (Pre-School) Regulations 2006, an 'overnight pre-school service' means a service in which pre-school children are cared for for a total of more than two hours between the hours of 7pm and 6am, except where the exemptions provided in Section 58 of the Childcare Act 1991 apply.

In addition to the National Standards for Pre-School Services 2010, the following standards apply in relation to overnight pre-school services.

Child Protection

There should be a written code of conduct/child protection policy specifically relating to overnight services. The policy should provide clear guidance for staff in relation to the physical contact considered appropriate for night-time routines and when attending to the children's hygiene needs. This policy should be made available to parents or guardians.

Care Policy

Details of the general night-time care policy should be documented. The following points must be taken into consideration.

- Information regarding television or video viewing
- Children's privacy in relation to personal hygiene, bathing, showering, dressing/undressing and sleeping location in relation to other children and staff
- Arrangements in relation to emergency contacts, e.g. full details for two recommended contacts should be supplied
- Behaviour management if a child fails to settle to sleep or becomes distressed (including procedures regarding bed-wetting, nightmares or general distress)
- Methods for monitoring sleeping children
- Methods for children's access to staff during the night.

Sleep Facilities

- The sleeping area for overnight care should be separate from the play, recreation and living areas.
- Each child should be provided with a separate and comfortable bed (or cot for children aged 0–2). Bunk beds are not deemed safe for children aged 0–8.
- In general, children aged 6 and upwards should sleep in same-gender rooms. However, where the overnight service is catering for more than one child from the same family, the parents can be consulted as to their preference in this regard.

Adult–Child Ratio

The recommended adult–child ratios for overnight services are:

- 0–1 year   1:3
- 1–6 years   1:5.

At least one member of staff should be awake and actively supervising and checking on the children at all times.

General Points

- The provider should work closely with parents in relation to children's needs before, during and after sleep.
- The service's insurance policy should provide cover for overnight services.
- Separate sleeping accommodation should be provided for staff.
- All doors and windows should be appropriately locked, taking fire safety considerations into account. The security system should be working.
- Advice should be sought from an appropriately qualified person regarding fire safety in overnight services.
- Children should have access to a telephone.

(National Standards for Pre-School Services 2010: 36–7)

Appendix 8: Referencing

If you are quoting directly from a source (e.g. a textbook), you must quote the text accurately, word for word. Enclose the quote within quotation marks.

If you are quoting a small amount of text, you can blend the original quotation into your own text, marking it off with quotation marks. For example:

> In my observation, TC took four short steps from the activity table to the bean bag. This is usual for this age group, since 'when infants learn to walk, they typically take small steps because of their limited balance control and strength' (Santrock 2009: 158).

If you are quoting a larger amount of text, it should be presented as a paragraph on its own. It should be *indented* in order for it to stand out; because of this, it does not need quotation marks.

If you do not quote a sentence in full, you must indicate this with the use of an *ellipsis*. For example:

> The motor accomplishments of the first year bring increasing independence, allowing infants to explore their environment more extensively and to initiate interactions with others more readily... (Santrock 2009: 159).

If you want to mention an author's idea as part of your sentence, but you do not want to use their words exactly, this is called a *citation*. This means that you acknowledge (cite) the author in your main text and give a full reference for their work at the end of your essay. For example:

> Santrock (2009) believes that because infants have limited balance control and strength, they typically take small steps while learning to walk.

If you want to cite a book that was written by many authors, it might be easiest to use *et al.* in the main text and give a full citation (that includes all of the authors) in the references at the end of your essay. For example:

> Parental participation leads to higher adult expectations and increased parental confidence and aspirations (Schweinhart et al. 2005).

Ensure that you quote and cite correctly throughout your essay. Then, at the end of your essay, you must provide a section called References. It is here that you give full publication details for any work you have quoted or cited. Again, it is worthwhile to examine published books on the subject of ECEC, so that you can see how references are displayed.

An example of a reference for a *book* is:

Healy, J. and Spencer, M. (2008) *Surviving your Placement in Health and Social Care*. UK: Open University Press.

An example of a reference for a *book with a compiling editor* is:

Fink, J. (ed.) (2004), *Care: Personal Lives and Social Policy*. Bristol: The Open University/ The Policy Press.

An example of a reference for an essay in a *journal* is:

Anglin, J. (1992), 'How Staff Develop', *FICE Bulletin*, 6, 18–24.

It is also important to give proper references for any relevant material you view on the internet.

Within your essay, you might want to refer the reader to a useful website. If so, give the website address in full. For example:

La Leche League of Ireland gives useful information on their website: www.lalecheleagueireland.com.

If you cite online material in the main body of your essay, give a full citation in the references at the end of your essay. Ensure that you include the date on which you accessed the online material. For example:

SESS (Special Education Support Service) 'Differentiation in the Classroom for Students with Special Educational Needs' (online) <www.sess.ie/resources/teaching-methods-and-organisation> accessed 13 June 2011.

There are many different referencing systems and it is worthwhile spending time in getting to know one suitable for your ECEC essays. The best way to do this is to look at published books in the area of ECEC. Take note of how references are used in these books. Pay attention to the use of commas, full stops, brackets and italics; they are important.

References and Further Reading

Beaver, M., Brewster, J., Jones, P., Lesley Keene, A., Neaum, S., Tallack, J., Green, S., Sheppard, H. and Walker, M. (2001) *Babies and Young Children: Diploma in Childcare and Education.* Cheltenham: Nelson Thornes.

Bruce, T. (2009) *Early Childhood: A Guide for Students* (2nd edn.). London: Sage.

CECDE (Centre for Early Childhood Development and Education) (2006) *Síolta: The National Quality Framework for Early Childhood Education.* Dublin: CECDE.

Daly, M., Byers, E. and Taylor, W. (2004) *Early Years Management in Practice.* Oxford: Heinemann.

Derman-Sparks, L. (1989) *Anti-Bias Curriculum: Tools For Empowering Young Children.* New York: National Association for the Education of Young Children.

DES (Department of Education and Science) (1999) *Ready to Learn – A White Paper on Early Childhood Education.* Dublin: Stationery Office.

DoHC (Department of Health and Children) (2000) *The National Children's Strategy. Our Children – Their Lives.* Dublin: Stationery Office.

DoHC (Department of Health and Children) (2004) *Food and Nutrition Guidelines for Pre-School Services.* Dublin: Stationery Office.

DoHC (Department of Health and Children) (2006) *Child Care (Pre-School Services) (No. 2) Regulations 2006 and Explanatory Guide to Requirements and Procedures for Notification and Inspection.* Dublin: Stationery Office. <http://www.dohc.ie/legislation/statutory_instruments/pdf/si20060604.pdf?direct=1> accessed August 2012.

DoHC (Department of Health and Children) (2010) *National Standards for Pre-School Services.* Dublin: DoHC. <http://www.dohc.ie/publications/pdf/natstandards_preschool.pdf?direct =1> accessed August 2012.

Dubowitz, Howard (1999) *Neglected Children: Research, Practice and Policy.* London: Sage Publications.

DYCA (Department of Children and Youth Affairs) (2011) *Children First: National Guidance for the Protection and Welfare of Children.* Dublin: Stationery Office.

Gibbs, G. (1998) *Learning By Doing: A Guide to Teaching and Learning.* London: FEU.

Jasper, M. (2003) *Beginning Reflective Practice.* Cheltenham: Nelson Thornes.

Lindon, J. (2002) *Childcare and Early Years Education.* London: Cengage Learning Vocational.

Murray, C. and Urban, M. (2012) *Diversity and Equality in Early Childhood.* Dublin: Gill & Macmillan.

NCCA (National Council for Curriculum and Assessment) (2009) *Aistear: The Early Childhood Curriculum Framework*. Dublin: NCCA.

OMC (Office of the Minister for Children) (2006) *National Childcare Strategy 2006–2010 Diversity and Equality Guidelines for Childcare Providers*. Dublin: OMC. <dcya.gov.ie> accessed September 2012.

OMC (Office of the Minister for Children) (2008) *National Childcare Strategy 2006–2010. National Guidelines for Childminders*. Dublin: OMC. <dcya.gov.ie> accessed September 2012.

Skuse, D. (1989) 'Emotional Abuse and Neglect', in R. Meadow (ed.), *ABC of Child Abuse*. London: British Medical Journal Publications.

Skuse, D. and Bentovim, A. (1994) 'Physical and Emotional Maltreatment', in M. Rutter, E. Taylor and L. Hersor (eds.), *Child and Adolescent Psychiatry* (3rd edn.). Oxford: Blackwell Scientific Publications.

Tassoni, P., Beith, K., Bulman, K. and Eldridge, H. (2007) *CACHE Level 3: Child Care and Education* (4th edn.). London: Heinemann.

Online Resources

Aistear

<www.ncca.biz/Aistear>

Barnardos

<www.barnardos.ie/assets/files/information-pack/Diversity_IP.pdf>: Diversity information pack.

Belbin Associates

<www.belbin.com/content/page/6133/Belbin(uk)-2011-TeamRolesInANutshell.pdf>: Team roles, according to Belbin.

Centre for Early Childhood Development and Education (CECDE)

<www.cecde.ie/gaeilge/pdf/Questions%20of%20Quality/Murray.pdf>: Éist project.

Childminding Ireland

<http://www.childmindingireland.ie>

Children's Rights Alliance

<www.childrensrights.ie/resources/18th-anniversary-ireland-ratifying-un-convention>: Ireland and the UNCRC.

Citizens Information

<www.citizensinformation.ie/en/>: The role of the Public Health Nurse.

Department of Children and Youth Affairs

<www.dcya.gov.ie/documents/childcare/diversity_and_equality.pdf>: Diversity and equality guidelines.

<www.dcya.gov.ie/viewdoc.asp?fn=/documents/childcare/CityCountyChildcareCommittee.htm>: City and County Childcare Committees (CCCs).

Department of Health and Children

<www.dohc.ie/legislation/statutory_instruments/pdf/si20060604.pdf?direct=1>: Child Care (Pre-School) Regulations 2006.

<www.dohc.ie/publications/children_first.html>: Children First: National Guidelines for the Protection and Welfare of Children.

< www.dohc.ie/publications/our_duty_to_care.html>: Our Duty to Care: The Principles of Good Practice for the Protection of Children and Young People.

<www.dohc.ie/publications/pdf/HPU_pre-school_guidelines.pdf?direct=1 <accessed>: Food and nutrition guidelines for pre-school children.

Department of Justice and Equality

<http://www.justice.ie/en/JELR/EqualStatusActsConsldtd_00_04.pdf/Files/EqualStatusActsConsldtd_00_04.pdf>: Equal Status Acts

<www.justice.ie/en/JELR/modelframework.pdf/Files/modelframework.pdf>: Developing Childcare in Ireland.

Diversity in Early Childhood Education and Training (DECET)

<www.decet.org/fileadmin/decet-media/publications/Diversity-and-Social-Inclusion.pdf>: Diversity and social inclusion.

Early Childhood Ireland

Forbairt Naíonraí Teoranta

<http://www.naionrai.ie>

Health Service Executive (HSE)

<www.hse.ie/eng/>

<www.healthpromotion.ie/hp-files/docs/HPM00406.pdf>: Infection in schools.

Meningitis Trust

<www.meningitis-trust.org>

National Association for the Education of Young Children

<www.naeyc.org/store/files/store/TOC/254.pdf>: Anti-bias education.

National Childminding Association, UK (NCMA)

<www.ncma.org.uk/pdf/being_reflective.pdf>: Being self-reflective.

Office of the Attorney General

<www.irishstatutebook.ie/1981/en/si/0390.html>: Infectious Diseases Regulations.

<www.irishstatutebook.ie/1991/en/act/pub/0017/index.html>: Childcare Act 1991.

<www.irishstatutebook.ie/1998/en/act/pub/0030/index.html>: Parental Leave Act 1998.

<www.irishstatutebook.ie/1998/en/act/pub/0049/index.html>: Safety, Health and Welfare at Work Act 2005.

<http://www.irishstatutebook.ie/2005/en/act/pub/0010/

Oireachtas

<www.oireachtas.ie/documents/bills28/acts/2004/A3004.pdf>: Education for Persons with Special Educational Needs Act 2004.

Organisation for Economic Co-operation and Development (OECD)

<www.oecd.org/education/preschoolandschool/34431749.pdf>: Background report of thematic review of ECEC in Ireland.

Síolta

<www.siolta.ie/media/pdfs/Research%20Djgest%20-%20Communication.pdf>

UNICEF

<http://www.unicef.org/crc/index_30177.html>: UNCRC.

Others

< www.teambuildingportal.com/articles/systems/practical-use-belbin-theory>: Building teams using Belbin's theory.

Index